The Coming Trials

SANE AND SENSIBLE PERSPECTIVES ON THE BOOK OF REVELATION

Prophecies of the Coming King, Vol. 1

STEVE EVANS

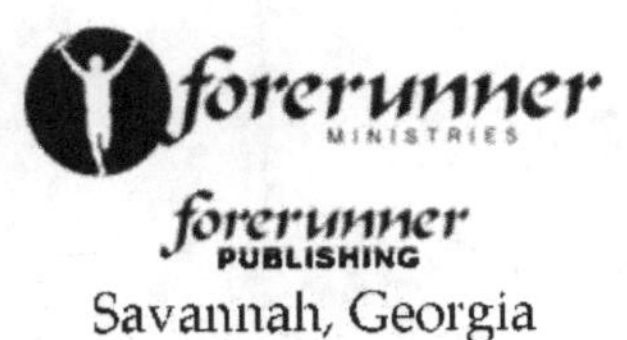

Savannah, Georgia

The Coming Trials
Prophecies of the Coming King, Vol. 1
2020 by Steve Evans

Distributed by Forerunner Ministries, Inc.
    4625 Sussex Place, Savannah, GA 31405
    Email: steve@forerunners4him.org
    Website: www.thelastdays.info

Published by Forerunner Ministries, Inc.
ISBN: 9798646890864
Imprint: Independently published

Cover and interior design by Forerunner Publishing, Savannah, Georgia.

Printed in the United States of America by Kindle Direct Publishing.

TABLE OF CONTENTS

START HERE

Are you ready for what's coming? This series will help you weather the storm!

The coming of our Lord Jesus Christ as an event that all Christians long to see but it is an event that is coming, not just as the appearance of a single Person, but as great waves of calamities, followed by matchless blessings. This series divides those flood waters into the Coming Trials, the Coming Judgments, and the Coming Chaos—calamities all; yet followed by the Coming Kingdom. The kingdom that our Lord Jesus brings with Him is absolutely astounding—well worth the pain and struggle that it will take to arrive at its gates. However, it will not come before the first three "comings" sweep savagely over the Earth.

Whatever book you presently have in your hand, you need to know that it is just one of four in a series that is incomplete without the other three. The Book of Revelation was given to us as a whole: It is a seamless, intricate, unfolding prophecy of the coming King. Yet, it naturally divides into four sections.

The Four "Comings"

The first section of the book is typically known as letters to the seven churches. These were actual churches in antiquity to which Jesus directed prophetic warnings. They're also (possibly) phases that the Church went through in its history. This backwards looking view relegates them safely to the past. What if they are predictions—prophetic forecasts—of the seven kinds of trials that will be coming to individuals and to churches in the Last Days? Then, they will be read in earnest by believers hoping to find how they can stay faithful in the Coming Trials and avoid drowning in the flood of judgments.

The Coming Judgments are only intended for unbelievers, but they will sweep up with them all unfaithful believers. We should read these with genuine and personal concern. May they inspire us to pray for the lost to be saved and to make sure that we (and our loved ones) don't fall into their ranks.

The third section includes those concurrent events that take place apart from the throne room in the Book of Revelation. They describe the players with whom we are most familiar: the dragon, the antichrist, the false prophet, fallen Babylon and the two witnesses. So, although the Coming Chaos is about activities, it also describes the actors within those events, or at their helm. This section reveals through whom the trials are coming and for whom the judgments are sent.

Finally, the Coming Kingdom describes the new heavenly order that automatically comes with Jesus when He returns. Indeed, He starts setting it into place immediately upon the successful completion of His war of conquest. With His judgment session and then through His millennial reign, that Kingdom extends way off into an unimaginable vision. Through John's eyes we catch tantalizing glimpses of a new Earth, a new Jerusalem, and hints of the delightful discoveries they contain. Unquestionably, our Lord has lavishly stored up treasures for all those who have loved His appearing and who remained faithful to Him through their trials.

I hope you will discover (as I did) that the Book of Revelation makes far more sense when viewed from these four perspectives. In truth, you may find yourself thinking time and again: How could it have been otherwise than what we are being shown here?

PROPHECIES
OF THE COMING KING
VOL. 1

The Coming Trials

And I tell you, you are Peter,
and on this rock I will build my church,
and the gates of hell shall not prevail against it.

Matthew 16:18

CHAPTER 1

THE SEVEN CHURCHES

Does it seem strange that the Book of Revelation which reveals our future began with letters to seven churches way back in the past? None of those churches are around anymore! Maybe that's the point. If they had heeded the sometimes-harsh warnings of their Lord, they just might have lasted all the way through to our day. Could faith and obedience change history to that degree? Our God calls us to be world changers, not those who are instead changed by the world as many of these believers were. Interestingly, this introduction to the Churches goes hand in hand with Jesus' stunning revelation of Himself to John on the Isle of Patmos. It is the revelation of Jesus Christ that changes us from "worldlings" into world changers. We will need both His past warnings and His present manifestations if we are to make it through the times coming upon us.

John to the seven churches that are in Asia: Grace to you and peace from him who is and who was and who is to come, and from the seven spirits who are before his throne, and from Jesus Christ the faithful witness, the firstborn of the dead, and the ruler of kings on earth. Revelation 1:4-5a

Why these Letters?

Is it possible that the letters to the Seven Churches are simply that? Or are they something more? How likely is it that when Jesus decided to give a world-class vision to John on Patmos that He just dropped these letters in because there was room in the satchel? Are they an afterthought? An "Oh, by the way, could you deliver these while you're at it?" appendage to the message that really mattered? That's possible, but scarcely believable. To unravel this tangle, we will have to look at the histories of these seven churches in Asia Minor and the characteristics of the Seven Churches in Revelation.

We have three possible ways of viewing these letters. First, they could simply be letters to seven individual churches that had issues back in the day. Jesus needed to address them, and we're given privileged insight to how He did it. End of story. Instructive, but mainly of historical importance. We can mine them for morals and principals like anything else in scripture, but that's it. There's no connection to church history or to the world's end. They're not part of the prophecy. They just got themselves tacked on. As straight-forward as this seems, very few of us want to leave it there. Nor should we.

These seven churches aren't haphazardly chosen for inclusion. They are on a kind of mail route that John's package of letters would have followed from Patmos to Ephesus, then up the coast past Smyrna to Pergamum before turning inland to Thyatira, Sardis, Philadelphia and finally Laodicea. There is an intentional, natural order to the letters. That's not surprising knowing our God. He does nothing by chance. This encourages us to believe that there is something more to these letters than meets the eye. Why were they chosen to send along with a prophecy about the End Times? Why were these cities providentially placed in this order?

A second trajectory, therefore, is to see the Seven Churches as representative of the Church Age. From the beginning of the age of grace right through to the end they give us a living picture of what the Church will be up against. Ephesus shows us the infant church facing the elementary struggle of discovering it must fight to maintain its first love—a fitting beginning for the Church at large and each of us as individuals. Other struggles and other stages of growth will ensue but finding a key to unlock their chosen order has been elusive. Pinning them on the known historical timeline of the Church universal is fraught with challenges, though it does seem that the first and last positions got it right. The lukewarmness of Laodicea is what much of the present-day church has decided to settle for in place of dynamic, self-sacrificial life. This approach is certainly possible but fails to deliver relevance for our time from all seven.

Instead of a sequence of successive church epochs, could it be that we are being shown something else, something of more universal application? A third possible interpretation is that these seven churches represent predicaments or problems that many churches will face worldwide in the Last Days. Not every church will face all seven of these trials, but all churches will face some of them. What's true for churches could also be true for individuals. The troubles, trials, and temptations these seven churches faced are things we can all expect to face going forward. Maybe not all of them, but enough to be thankful that we have read these letters and know what Jesus would want us to do to walk faithfully through them.

CHAPTER 2

THE VISITATION AT PATMOS

Revelation 1:1-20

John begins his extraordinary book in the customary manner of greeting the Seven Churches which will receive these letters. He also gives honor and praise to their common Lord. Finally, he introduces himself briefly (for they know him well). Then, he drops the hammer: Jesus visited Him! There he was on the Isle of Patmos filling the empty days of exile with worship, when totally out of the blue the very One he was worshipping appeared right in front of him. This wasn't quite the same gentle Teacher he had walked beside over sixty years earlier in distant Galilee. This was the awe-inspiring, fear-invoking Lord of the Universe—and He said He had messages for His Church. We have been unpacking those messages ever since.

When I saw him, I fell at his feet as though dead. But he laid his right hand on me, saying, "Fear not, I am the first and the last, and the living one. I died, and behold I am alive forevermore, and I have the keys of Death and Hades. Revelation 1:17-18

Summary of this Section

The commentary in these sections contain insights based on the text of scripture, not fabricated through speculation.[1] Speculation is trying to "see" more than we are being shown. What we see by biblical revelation is real enough, but a fuller view will only come as these still distant components draw nearer. Speculation can readily become a pathway for deception.

Of the many bizarre things and intriguing persons introduced to us in this opening Prologue to the Book of Revelation, one that could easily be overlooked is simply the number seven. But nothing is simple in these pages! There are seven churches, seven candle stands, seven stars, seven angels and "seven spirits who are before his throne" (quoted above). All these will need careful explaining, and fortunately some explanations will be given within the text itself. For other interpretations we will have to look elsewhere. That's where the work begins. That work, in turn, can lead to the thrill of discovery, but also to the danger of misdirection. It's best with this book to take careful steps, rather than great leaps of faith. Many fall off this mountain when racing to get too quick a glimpse or too far-sighted a view of the future.

The flurry of sevens should draw our attention to several things. First, nothing is left to chance. It cannot be an accident that there are so many sevens right at the beginning of the Revelation. Seven is the number of completion and rest—God rested on the seventh day after His six-day work week of creation. Hence, things that seem strange or attention getting—like so many sevens—may likely also carry a symbolic meaning. This doesn't mean that we will be able to figure everything out, but it puts us on notice that prophecy is the language of imagery and metaphor.

Sometimes the biblical text will tell us when it is being symbolic. Sometimes it won't. In that aspect it is also dreamlike. Indeed, prophecy often gets mentioned in direct connection with dreams which are also a means through which it is frequently received. Dreams are notoriously difficult to decipher. They don't follow proper timelines. Geography also can easily lose its customary boundaries. Take care. Pray much. And listen well. One thing is certain: We need His revelations to understand Revelation. Fortunately, Jesus already gave us a major "key" to interpretation. It is to listen with a heart to obey what we hear. To the one who "keeps" his words (by obeying them), Jesus reveals even more of Himself and that necessarily includes His truths.

Whoever has my commandments and keeps them, he it is who loves me. And he who loves me will be loved by my Father, and I will love him and manifest [reveal] myself to him." John 14:21

Pre-Figured in Scripture

Many elements of the Book of Revelation have already "appeared" in the biblical prophetic narrative in the past, somewhat like a dress rehearsal for the final drama. These foreshadows are called "types" because they precede their ultimate expression (the "antitype").[2] As shadows of the future reality, however, they cast a revealing light of their own.

1. The Jerusalem Council Letter

The first record we have of any letter to any church is one that earns three favorable mentions in the Book of Acts—the Jerusalem's Council's letter concerning a decision they made. That should alert us to its importance. The Great Commission is only given twice.[3] The Great Commandments, as great as they are, are given only three times. The contents of this letter are repeated verbatim three times![4] Even Paul's letter to the Galatians seems to refer to the incident that provoked the writing of this letter.[5] How important are letters in the New Testament? Extremely. The wonderful thing about this letter is that it was written entirely as an encouragement to lessen the yoke of the Jewish Law from the shoulders of the new Gentile believers. As such it was received with gladness.[6]

Then it seemed good to the apostles and the elders, with the whole church, to choose men from among them and send them to Antioch with Paul and Barnabas. They sent Judas called Barsabbas, and Silas, leading men among the brothers, with the following letter: "The brothers, both the apostles and the elders, to the brothers who are of the Gentiles in Antioch and Syria and Cilicia, greetings. Acts 15:22-23

One difference between this letter and the letters to the Seven Churches is that the Jerusalem Council was sending out an encyclical—a letter for wide or general distribution. It was intended to be read by all Gentile churches everywhere, because it addressed the issue of what they should obey from God's Law in order to be members in good standing in the eyes of the Jewish Christian believers who led the young Church. The letters to the Seven Churches, on the other hand, carry specifics which apply only to those churches. Or do they? The other difference between the Jerusalem's Council's letter and those of Jesus is the reprimands and warnings He gave. We would be wise to "listen in" on the conversation and glean insights for ourselves from others that Jesus had to correct. God willing, this will help us avoid their disastrous mis-steps—and spare us from the consequences.

2. The Apostolic Letters

We may not typically think of it this way, but two thirds of the New Testament began life as letters to churches—not as books of scripture. Personal letters in our day are rare. They were back then too. The difference is that we have so many other effective ways of communicating to people at a distance. Nevertheless, any missionary can tell you how precious words from home are when set on paper and received by (infrequent) mail. You know that a lot of thought went into them—unlike most cell phone texts. You know that the person who sent it really cares about you—otherwise, why take the trouble? Best of all, you can pull the letter out and go over it again and again.

The letters of scripture work the same way. We pull them out and go over them endlessly, because the One who sent them really, really loves us. And we relive that love as we reread the letters. Even so, sometimes even perfect love must send words of correction. Paul hated to include that part of the message, but he loved too deeply to gloss over things. He knew that if they weren't addressed, they would bring more lasting harm than the passing pain of being brought to attention. Peter and James followed suit. It is completely in line with this apostolic "tradition" that Jesus will later write His own letters to seven churches through John. Here is how Paul put it.

For this reason I write these things while I am away from you, that when I come I may not have to be severe in my use of the

authority that the Lord has given me for building up and not for tearing down. 2 Corinthians 13:10

Revealed by Scripture

The Bible exposes the secret plans and deceptive operations of the dark kingdom, even as it unveils the glorious realities of what our God is doing. The truths of scripture are, therefore, our rock-solid building blocks for interpreting the times we are entering. Nevertheless, for biblical information to become true revelation both prayer and the Holy Spirit are needed.

This introduction to the letters for the Seven Churches also includes an opening explanation for what this book is intended to be and how John came to receive its messages. It also introduces us to the ultimate Revealer: Jesus. You won't want to miss that part. It's a showstopper!

1. John's Introduction and Blessing

1 The revelation of Jesus Christ, which God gave him to show to his servants the things that must soon take place. He made it known by sending his angel to his servant John, 2 who bore witness to the word of God and to the testimony of Jesus Christ, even to all that he saw. Revelation 1:1-2

As John begins writing his book, the first thought that he wants to convey is that everything which follows will be "the revelation of Jesus Christ." This is a phase with at least two meanings since the absence of the preposition "of" in the text opens a door to a double entendre. This book will be a revealing *of* Jesus Christ—unveiling to us hidden things about His purpose and destiny yet to be fulfilled. It will also be a revelation *from* Jesus to His Church—manifesting to us hidden things about our own future destiny and purpose in the plan of God. In all honesty, the latter sense probably drives most of us into studying this book, though the former meaning may be the one primarily intended. Happily, we don't have to choose between either interpretation, but can readily embrace both.

The order of transmission is fascinating, because we must back up the revelation to God the Father who initiated it. Before these words and visions could be given to us, they had to first be revealed to Jesus. Recall that while on earth, Jesus disclosed that the timing of His Return was unknown to Him.[7] Other things may have been hidden from His sight as well while He walked among us. Now—while His beloved disciple still drew breath—He received further revelation. It is this new understanding of the Father's secret plan that Jesus wants to make known to us. Accordingly, He transmits what He's been shown to "his angel" who will be passing it on to John. But the chain of divine delivery will not end there. Under the inspiration of the Holy Spirit, John will pass it on to all of us through the book he soon writes.

John will now be a faithful "witness" on our behalf concerning three things. He will convey accurately to us "the Word of God" which he heard spoken about these events. Those words include "the testimony of Jesus Christ" which (as we have seen) indicates both truths about Jesus as well as truths testified to by Jesus Himself. Here John uses the divine title, Christ ("Messiah"), so that there could be no doubt in anyone's mind that this is the same Jesus whom John knew in the flesh who is in truth the earth's Savior and Lord. This is after all the same John who in his letter warned us all to "test the spirits" since many antichrists and false prophets have "gone out into the world."[8] We will certainly hear more about them in the chapters to come! Finally, John will hold nothing back but will convey every detail, "even to all that he saw."

This "angel" deserves special attention. It is widely believed that the person Jesus sent to John with the Revelation was a celestial being, an angel in the ordinary sense we understand the term. The term angel, however, is a job description. It means messenger. Naturally, we think immediately of the heavenly host, but there are other glorious beings in heaven than those spirits who have always lived in the unseen realm. The redeemed are also there. This is a reality that even John had to receive correction about—and wanted us to remember it as well. John tells us twice that "the messenger" reprimanded him (once) for bowing towards him, declaring himself to be "a fellow servant with you and your brothers the prophets."[9] Would a holy angel consider himself a "fellow servant"? The Word declares them to be our servants for the sake of the gospel.[10] They also know that we have been placed below them only "for a little while," but our destined position is higher.[11] Is it possible, then, that this unnamed messenger is one of the redeemed? Not only that, but might he have been a former ("fellow") prophet while living on the earth?

Blessed is the one who reads aloud the words of this prophecy, and blessed are those who hear, and who keep what is written in it, for the time is near. Revelation 1:3

What an encouragement this passage is! Just by reading these words aloud a blessing is guaranteed to come. That's good because (as we know) understanding the words of this book is a much more difficult task. Even so, for those who press in not only to hear, but to "keep what is written," a further blessing is pronounced. Keeping God's Word requires understanding it in order to obey it. Towards that end, both the messenger and John will provide insights and explanations as we go along. The full weight of interpretation, of course, depends upon us—upon our willingness to give it the effort as well as our openness "to hear" what the Spirit is saying as opposed to what we might prefer.

These pronounced blessings are punctuated with a sense of urgency "for the time is near." So, begins the first of several ironic announcements that we'll receive which reveal the wide difference between our Lord's sense of "soon" and ours. No doubt, every generation of believers that took these words to heart was somehow prepared by them for what they would undergo in their lifetime. Nevertheless, those generations did not see the prophesied Day draw "near." We will. How much more, therefore, should we press in for the blessing of "keeping" these words? What is revealed here will go a long way towards keeping us faithful in our steps and full of faith in our hearts as we enter the days that are coming.

2. John's Greeting to the Seven Churches

4 John to the seven churches that are in Asia: Grace to you and peace from him who is and who was and who is to come, and from the seven spirits who are before his throne, 5a and from Jesus Christ the faithful witness, the firstborn of the dead, and the ruler of kings on earth. Revelation 1:4-5a

In this opening portion of the book, John now addresses "the seven churches that are in Asia." Asia identifies the Roman province which occupied the area now held by the modern nation of Turkey. The Seven Churches are not the only churches in Asia, but they are the ones singled out by Jesus for individual attention. Whatever else may follow, the Lord wants His churches to receive grace and peace "from Him." That's good to know because if we've read ahead, we also know that strong words of rebuke and correction will follow. Nevertheless, the foundation for all of God's dealings with us is grace, leading to peace—full restoration of fellowship between God and us.

This greeting isn't being sent from Jesus alone, but also from the "seven spirits who are before his throne." These are seven celestial beings who are the angels associated with the Seven Churches as we'll learn later. For now, their unexplained inclusion alerts us to the ongoing reality that much of this revelation will need revealing! Jesus, however, hardly needs an introduction, though He gets one and a fine one it is. He is the "faithful witness" whom John seeks to mirror as he bears his own witness of Jesus. Jesus is also "the firstborn of the dead" who raised John (and us) to new life from the living death of sin. He will also raise us beyond death into heavenly life when that time comes—a necessary ability which we'll need Him to exercise in the context of the millions of deaths about to be prophesied. Perhaps this manner of greeting is, therefore, meant as an encouraging reminder that although the kings of the earth will be arrayed against Him in the end, Jesus is unquestionably the "ruler of kings of the earth."

5b To him who loves us and has freed us from our sins by his blood 6 and made us a kingdom, priests to his God and Father, to him be glory and dominion forever and ever. Amen. Revelation 1:5b-6

Don't you love John's heart? He is only a few steps into the Revelation, but he stops to interrupt his own prologue with praise. This glorious Person who "loves us and has freed us" deserves to be glorified with thanksgiving at every mention of His saving deeds. At unspeakable cost to Himself, Jesus saved us "by His blood" for only His death could free us from what our sins required. But He didn't stop there. By His grace He "made us"—the corrupt ones who worshipped the god of this world—a kingdom of holy priests who now serve the true and living God. Such a gracious and magnificent Being deserves to be glorified as He reigns "forever and ever." Amen!

Behold, he is coming with the clouds, and every eye will see him, even those who pierced him, and all tribes of the earth will wail on account of him. Even so. Amen. Revelation 1:7

Let's cut to the chase. Jesus is not content to reign only from heaven. He is determined to also reign on earth! That's what this Book of Revelation—His revelation—reveals. He is "coming with the clouds" to invade earth, not as the usurper Satan did by stealth in the Garden. No, earth's rightful sovereign is returning in such a way that "every eye will see him." This will be a welcomed sight for the faithful who "love to see His appearing" whether it is by the Daystar rising in our hearts, or before our yearning eyes when the great Day dawns.[12]

Sadly, His Return will bring deep sorrow to those whose desires took them in a different direction. Foremost among this mournful group will be the as yet unconverted Jews. "Those who pierced Him" speaks of the sword's piercing long ago at the cross, but also hints of their heart-piercing rejection of Him as their Messiah for the past two thousand years. These "lost" tribes of Israel will themselves be pierced by the appalling realization of how great their apostasy has been. Other lost ones, who will "wail on account of Him," will include "all tribes of the earth." How they will wish it to be other than it is on that Day. "Even so," it is what it is.

"I am the Alpha and the Omega," says the Lord God, "who is and who was and who is to come, the Almighty." Revelation 1:8

We began with John's description of this coming King. Now, Jesus steps into the prophesy with a personally delivered declaration: "I am the Alpha and the Omega." He is the beginning and the end of this story and of all stories. He is the Creator who set everything in motion, though an enemy derailed the original plan. Even so, He is the Redeemer who will bring everything into alignment with His eternal purposes. He not only "is" the great I AM of Exodus fame; He is the One who "was" as He died our death and the One who "is to come" upon His Return. He not only knows the end from the beginning, but He declares it to us with absolute assurance in the prophecies to come. Such a masterful Person can only be described as "the Almighty." Get ready earth. Take cover lords of the earth. You are about to meet more than your match!

3. John's Vision of the Son of Man

I, John, your brother and partner in the tribulation and the kingdom and the patient endurance that are in Jesus, was on the island called Patmos on account of the word of God and the testimony of Jesus. Revelation 1:9

With his description of the Main Character completed, John takes a moment to introduce himself. Hardly a bit player in this drama, John doesn't seek to upstage us. He's one of us—our "brother and partner" in this great enterprise of faith. Well, that's not quite what he said, though it is a part of what he means. This letter is exclusively being written to fellow believers, not to outsiders. This is not for evangelism, though some have tried to use it that way. No, the gospel is for evangelism. John's already written one of those.

This Revelation is for preparing the saints to be saints—to stay holy and steadfast when the going gets tough. And tough it's going to be. According to this we are those who will partner with him "in the tribulation" to come. That's not what we want to hear even though he assures us that through this we will share with him in the "kingdom"—our Lord's ultimate reign. Nevertheless, we know (as he reminds us) that for us to see that kingdom come, we will need all the "patient endurance" that is in Jesus. Fortunately for us, all that is in Jesus can also become ours through faith. We'll need it.

John isn't speaking of tribulation as an armchair theologian. He knows first-hand what it means to go through tribulation, being currently exiled on the prison island of Patmos. The essence of tribulation is persecution "on account of the world of God and the testimony of Jesus." The dark powers of the world do not want the truth to come to light for anyone or by anyone. John's tribulation is a foreshadow in his time of the darkness which will come when worldwide persecution of Christians and Jews covers the earth. We will need the same "patient endurance" he did.

10 I was in the Spirit on the Lord's day, and I heard behind me a loud voice like a trumpet 11 saying, "Write what you see in a book and send it to the seven churches, to Ephesus and to Smyrna and to Pergamum and to Thyatira and to Sardis and to Philadelphia and to Laodicea." Revelation 1:10-11

Despite being in exile far removed from those he loved, there is still One he loves more than any other. Rather than giving way to depression, John moved into worship and found himself "in the Spirit" one undated Sunday ("the Lord's day"). It was then, that he first heard the celestial summons. How could he have missed it? This wasn't the whisper to "come up higher" we may hear in our quiet times. This was "a loud voice" that broke through his worship with a resounding blast "like a trumpet." Did it startle him? He didn't see it coming—the sudden, unexpected address came from "behind." No doubt he spun around. Such a summons can't be played with as we see emphasized by the language of command. John is to "write" what he sees and "send" it, presumably without delay to all seven of the churches mentioned. John's willing obedience is foreknown and fully expected.

12 Then I turned to see the voice that was speaking to me, and on turning I saw seven golden lampstands, 13 and in the midst of the lampstands one like a son of man, clothed with a long robe and with a golden sash around his chest. Revelation 1:12-13

Who is it who issues such a demand? John says he "turned to see the voice." This may indicate that at this moment he wasn't yet sure that he would see the visible appearance of the one speaking to him. Perhaps, he had encounters like this in the past. Most scholars and church tradition agree that this exile happened near the end of Emperor Domitian's reign—96 AD. That would put John somewhere in his eighties, if indeed he was recruited by Jesus as a young man over 66 years earlier. Such a long and storied career would have given the prophet countless opportunities for angelic and divine visitations. Such things are not uncommon in the biblical accounts or even today in many lives.

What he sees first are seven "golden lampstands" which symbolize the Seven Churches. Then, he discerns a living presence "in the midst of the lampstands." He looks "like a son of man" which we may take as a code name for Jesus, but that isn't what John says. He knows exactly what Jesus looks like. Even after all the years, even without any intervening visitations, how could he ever lose the indelible impression of that Face? As with so many other things in this Revelation, that which is initially unclear will come better into view through passages that follow. At this point all that John knows is that this person doesn't appear to be angelic, but human—like a son of man. Even so, he is robed in heavenly attire wearing "a long robe and with a golden sash around his chest." Still, it could be anyone. But with a voice such as John first heard, this is clearly someone of otherworldly stature.

14 The hairs of his head were white, like white wool, like snow. His eyes were like a flame of fire, 15 his feet were like burnished bronze, refined in a furnace, and his voice was like the roar of many waters. Revelation 1:14-15

Reading ahead, we know who this is—it's Jesus. No surprise for us. John, however, follows the clues just as we will when such a moment comes to us. His eyes travel from what we could call the universal clothing of heaven, to personal features that now seem more angelic than human. Moving from the outside in and from top to bottom, John sees hair "like white wool" as pure as snow (or as that of an unblemished lamb?). Next, he describes eyes "like a flame of fire" which speaks of holiness, combined with the intensity of a blazing passion.

This incredible person has feet that convey an impression of stupendous strength. "Like burnished bronze" tells us that in addition to being powerful, they shine with a heavenly brilliance. That they have been "refined in a furnace" give us an important clue to the identity of this person who appears both human and divine. He walked through a refiner's fire and passed the test. Earth alone is the domain for testing the metal of one's character. Such an ordeal would give authority and depth to anyone's voice. His is "like the roar of many waters"—commanding, all-engulfing, over-whelming. These signs show us that his was not an ordinary human test.

In his right hand he held seven stars, from his mouth came a sharp two-edged sword, and his face was like the sun shining in full strength. Revelation 1:16

John gazes (in wonder? or dread?) as he sees that this glorious being holds "seven stars" in his right hand alone. No time to process any of this, his eyes—transfixed by the heavenly vision—must move on. Astoundingly, a sharp, two-edged sword thrusts forth "from his mouth." The Word of God is a sword that cuts two ways: It condemns to judgment those who reject eternal truth and liberates those who receive it. By this we see at last that this person is no "mere" angelic messenger, but the Source of Wisdom—the eternal Word which John had earlier written about in the Prologue to his gospel.[13] Perhaps, it is as this recognition is dawning in the beloved disciple's mind, that the Person before him is transfigured: The image that had earlier seemed like a son of man, now has a "face like the sun shining in full strength." Where have we seen that before? John saw it with his own eyes on the Mount of Transfiguration.[14] The identification is complete.

17 When I saw him, I fell at his feet as though dead. But he laid his right hand on me, saying, "Fear not, I am the first and the last, 18 and the living one. I died, and behold I am alive forevermore, and I have the keys of Death and Hades. Revelation 1:17-18

Can we imagine the shaft of uncreated light which now pierced John's vision? In an instant, his memory is alive to what he along with Peter and James saw on the holy mountain in Galilee so many decades earlier. In the same instant, he is seeing the wondrous sight in front of him in real time. Here is the glorious God-Man in full, otherworldly display. Is it any wonder that he "fell at his feet as though dead"? We would too, though it does seem strange that one of the last times we "saw" John, he was leaning his head in perfect peace upon the breast of the very One he cannot gaze upon now. This is not to imply that John ever became complacent, but lest we get too familiar with the "friendly" side of Jesus, we would do well to remember that this is the One who makes the pillars of heaven quake. One look upon His unveiled countenance… Well, let's thank God that He knows how much we can bear and that the Blood—His own Blood—covers us.

It is exactly this that Jesus recalls to John's memory. He lays "his right hand" on John, a gesture that draws upon the frequent mention in scripture of God's right hand of salvation.[15] Immediately, Jesus reminds John of what He has done for Him (and for us). It is as if He is saying, "John, take courage. It's Me, Jesus. Remember? I'm the One who 'died' (you were there) and 'behold' (look at Me now) 'I am alive forevermore.' So, fear not!" Though He died, He remains "the living one." Indeed, the writer of Hebrews tells us that Jesus gained His priesthood by "the power of an indestructible life."[16] Further, Peter declared to the crowds at Pentecost that it was "impossible" for Jesus to "be held" by death.[17] To top it off, Jesus announces to John that He holds "the keys of Death and Hades." This is the God we are going to need going forward! Whatever these prophecies will say about our future, no matter how bleak it may appear, Jesus holds the keys. He is in us; He is with us; and if we are in Him, our future is secure.

4. John's Commission to Write this Book

19 Write therefore the things that you have seen, those that are and those that are to take place after this. 20 As for the mystery of the seven stars that you saw in my right hand, and the seven golden lampstands, the seven stars are the angels of the seven churches, and the seven lampstands are the seven churches. Revelation 1:19-20

Finally, comes the commission: "Write, therefore." Based on what he now sees in Jesus, based on what will be shown to him, John is to write about "those things that are." There is much in Revelation about the times John lives in. There is also a great deal—in fact far more—about "those things that are to take place after this." Unquestionably, Revelation is a revelation of the future, both for the world (which will be judged) and for believers (who will be liberated). Even the parts that were addressed to the past—the present time of John's day—will have seed lessons in them that will be important for us to harvest in our day.

Almost as an afterthought, Jesus decides to clear up some mysteries. The seven stars are "the angels of the seven churches." The seven golden lampstands represent "the seven churches" to whom the letters will be addressed. Why Jesus likes being so mysterious must be part of what it means to be the greatest Enigma ever. We need to get used to this. Only parts of the End Times puzzle will be revealed to us as we go along. We see dimly.[18] Even if we are diligent at assembling the parts, we should expect that many pieces of revelation will be withheld until the right time. That is something which cannot be forced. It may be our "glory" to search a matter out, but it is Jesus' prerogative to conceal it.

It is the glory of God to conceal things, but the glory of kings is to search things out. Proverbs 25:2

CHAPTER 3

THE FIRST CHURCH: EPHESUS

Revelation 2:1-7

The Ephesian believers were like many of us. They had a sharp eye out for anything that smacked of deception or false doctrine. Jesus assured them that was good, nevertheless… That's where the comparison gets scary. Despite their watchfulness against wrong thinking, their hearts had grown cold. Which matters more to the Lord: great head knowledge or a heart on fire with passion for Him? When we put it that way the answer is obvious, and the choice is clear. But real life is a murky business, where the cares of this world can easily overtake the good seed—without us ever noticing a thief of hearts came in to steal ours.

"To the angel of the church in Ephesus write… I know you are enduring patiently... But I have this against you, that you have abandoned the love you had at first. Revelation 2:1, 3-4

Chief Characteristics

Travelers, commerce and correspondence from Greece or Italy would arrive at Asia Minor's major seaport, Ephesus, then journey up the coast towards Pergamum, before turning east on the interior highway to Laodicea. The letter to the church at Ephesus would have been the first letter delivered.

Ephesus is a seaport on the western coast of modern Turkey, the most prosperous of all the seven cities which received letters. In the first century under Emperor Augustus, Ephesus became the leading city of the Roman province of Asia. It held great importance as both a commercial and cultural center with monumental buildings, a library, aqueducts and baths rivaling those of Rome itself. The grandest structure of all was the Temple of Artemis, patroness of fertility, whose magnificent abode was one of the seven wonders of the world and a pilgrimage point for pagan worshippers throughout the Empire. It is to the embattled church in this hotbed of worldly attraction that Jesus directs His first letter.

Pre-Figured in Scripture

King Solomon Lost His First Love

How did it happen? The wisest of men become one of the most foolish. Centuries earlier, Esau traded his inheritance for a bowl of porridge (lentil stew).[1] Solomon traded his for the sake of his many wives. No doubt it seemed to Solomon like he'd made a better bargain than Esau. Until you remember Eternity. That's what the once-wise king wrote that God placed in our hearts.[2] He put it there so that when the trial came, we would have a marker to show where the line was drawn. We could remember that there was a "first love" we owed allegiance—a love more giving, more deserving and more commanding than any of the other loves. This is what Jesus called the Ephesian church to recover. Solomon lost his first love. Jesus wants the Ephesians to get theirs back.

For when Solomon was old his wives turned away his heart after other gods, and his heart was not wholly true to the LORD his God, as was the heart of David his father. 1 Kings 11:4

Revealed by Scripture

To the Church in Ephesus

"To the angel of the church in Ephesus write: 'The words of him who holds the seven stars in his right hand, who walks among the seven golden lampstands. Revelation 2:1

The opening address of this first letter to the Seven Churches is directed to "the angel of the church in Ephesus." This cannot mean that only an angelic dignitary from the unseen realm is the intended recipient, since the rest of the letter makes it clear that

Jesus is sending both encouragement and correction to the church's Christian believers. It does, however, reveal to us that this church has an angel who is over it in some ordained role: as a watchman, a helper or guardian, or a ministering spirit.[3] In fact, according to Jesus' previous greeting to John, we know that all seven of the Churches have their own angel.[4] Does this mean that every Christian church everywhere also has its own angel? Due to silence on this point, it is impossible to say from scripture one way or the other, although the likely supposition would be that this is indeed the case, since God shows no partiality.[5] What then is our protocol for addressing them? What are their proper responsibilities over us and what are ours to them? More silence!

What Jesus does provide is a revelation of Himself. These words are from Him—the One "who holds" and the One "who walks." As Lord of All, Jesus holds the seven stars (the seven angels) in His powerful "right hand" of salvation.[6] Imagine holding seven celestial beings in one hand. His hand is mighty! He reaches through these lofty "stars"—His loyal agents—to carrying out His and the Father's great plan of redemption. As "the Great Shepherd of the Sheep" Jesus walks among the seven golden lampstands (the Seven Churches) to watch over them and care for their every need.[7] Is there a veiled reference here to that other watcher who "walked to and fro upon the earth"?[8] That one walked—"prowled" would be a better word—not with the intent of caring for the sheep as a good shepherd would, but devouring them.[9] We will see far more of him later.

2 "I know your works, your toil and your patient endurance, and how you cannot bear with those who are evil, but have tested those who call themselves apostles and are not, and found them to be false. 3 I know you are enduring patiently and bearing up for my name's sake, and you have not grown weary. Revelation 2:2-3

Isn't it wonderful that Jesus knows of our works? Even a cup of water given from a good heart doesn't go unnoticed by our God.[10] Striving to be good by our own efforts may still amount to only filthy rags, but that which we do under His leadership and by His Spirit are seen as good "works" by our Lord.[11] Jesus calls it work because the way of faith at times requires "toil" and the resolute effort of "patient endurance" to withstand the Enemy's attacks. Just what John previously warned of in his own first letter to all the churches, Jesus now describes as having happened here in Ephesus.[12]

False teachers with the temerity to "call themselves apostles" crept in. Seeking to camouflage themselves as leaders hand-picked by the Good Shepherd, they nevertheless proved to be wolves instead. Fortunately, they were noticed and "tested" by the faithful whose zeal is such that they "cannot bear" with those who are shown to be servants of the evil one by their works. Jesus praises them for "bearing up" well under this assault and for not growing weary despite the toil required to endure it patiently. He knows that they did it for His "name's sake"—out of a pure motive to honor Him. No one prizes such covenant loyalty more than our God.

But I have this against you, that you have abandoned the love you had at first. Revelation 2:4

Considering the foregoing praise and encouragement, this verse comes as the shock it is intended to be. It is a hammer blow to spiritual complacency struck by a master Carpenter. Complacency is that state of mind in which we imagine that all is well because we seem to be doing well. There is a blessing of God upon our good works which is only right—He is a rewarder—but it carries an often-unnoticed snare. Walking in blessings from the Lord is not the same thing as being a blessing to the Lord. There was a time in Jacob's later life when God had fully satisfied his heart, but he had not yet satisfied God's heart. Accordingly, the Lord called him to resume the faith-journey by going to Bethel and building an altar there.[13]

Altars speak of worship, of putting the Lord first, of warming our hearts with the fire of first love, kindled afresh with sacrifice devoted to Him alone. This the blessed and zealous Ephesians failed to do. Like the seed in the third stage of

Jesus' parable, the legitimate cares of this world had somehow claimed their care and attention—and carried their hearts away from the One who called them to work. Can we do that? Can we become so caught up serving the Lord of the Harvest that we lose the true harvest? Paul warned us that even if we are so zealous that we give our bodies "to be burned" it will count as nothing if the fire of love goes out.[14] But we didn't need Paul to reveal that. Jesus did when He placed the command to love God first—well ahead of loving and serving others.

Remember therefore from where you have fallen; repent, and do the works you did at first. If not, I will come to you and remove your lampstand from its place, unless you repent. Revelation 2:5

If you are fortunate enough to hear a divine warning, there's still time to do something about it. We often shout belatedly to someone "Watch out!" once they've already stepped off a curb and stumbled. Our Lord sees trouble coming and sends His Word with time to spare. He knows that these poor Ephesians aren't even aware of what they've lost.[15] The art of deception which the Enemy practices works by stealing in unnoticed and "spiriting off" the best goods with no one left any the wiser. If these words of Jesus sound strong, it's because the deceived are sound asleep and need a good shout to awaken them.

With the warning shout comes the pathway of restoration: "Remember… repent, and do the works you did at first." Remembrance is practically the whole of it. The spiritual masters of days gone by called it "recollection"—the necessary, daily process of recalling heart and mind to focus upon our divine Lover.[16] Collect your wayward thoughts and re-center all on Him. With recollection comes remembrance. We remember what it felt like when we were closer—how our "hearts burned within us."[17] Then, grace happens as we re-member by joining our body back to its rightful Head. "Repent and do the work" too often makes us think of religious activity when really it is a matter of the heart. It takes a work of faith for the heart to believe the gospel's promise of a love far greater than our failings. This is just the work that Jesus said we "must do."[18] He expects us to put our backs to it—the devil is playing for keeps and we should too.

To spur the newly awakened sleepers to truly rise and shine, Jesus gives a second warning direr than the first. If they don't rekindle their first love, He will come and remove their "lampstand from its place." Each church represents a lampstand burning before the Lord as well as the world: "Let your light shine before others, so that they may see your good works and give glory to your Father."[19] If our works no longer shine as a light that attracts others to Christ, Jesus sees that the flame of our church's lampstand has gone out. He doesn't want to remove it, but He will—"unless" there is repentance. Grace gives us time. Repentance buys us time. May we never trade on grace thinking we can buy time indefinitely without fully repenting. Did the Ephesians repent? History records that Islamic invaders eventually swept Christianity away from what had once been its cradle.

Yet this you have: you hate the works of the Nicolaitans, which I also hate. Revelation 2:6

A second word of encouragement is given. It is a commonplace teaching nowadays to sandwich the meat of correction between morsels of praise. Did it begin here with Jesus' example of dealing with an errant church? This word plays upon the previous thoughts. Just as Jesus praised the work they had done (resisting false teachers) yet faulted the work they failed to do (keeping their first love alive), so now He praises their hatred for the failed "works of the Nicolaitans."

If we cannot love God as He desires at least we can hate as He hates. David boldly declared, "Do I not hate those who hate you? ...I hate them with complete hatred."[20] This is the man after God's heart, something Jesus wants the Ephesians to become.[21] The words of David, however, are not quite in keeping with the Spirit of the New Covenant expressed here by Jesus who doesn't hate the Nicolaitans, though He does hate their works. We would temper David's expression, but not his passion. Still, one wonders what those Nicolaitans are doing that is so hated by both Jesus and the Ephesian believers?

Unfortunately, we will have to keep wondering. There is no clear evidence coming to us from antiquity which can identify who the Nicolaitans are or what their false teaching contained. There are two currents of thought—guesses really. One is that their leader was a deacon named Nicolas (there is such a one mentioned in Acts 6:5) who possibly taught people to sin by eating food sacrificed to idols and by sexual immorality. The other is that the group's name derives from *nicolah*, a Greek word that means "let us eat" and likely indicated they encouraged the error of eating meat sacrificed to idols. You see the common thread: food, especially when contaminated as a ritual offering to false gods. How does this help us? It helps to know that even food can become a spiritual battleground. One of the strangest prophecies about the Last Days is that vegetarianism would abound.[22] How did Paul see that one coming?

Perhaps the best candidate for the Nicolaitan error is sexual immorality. This is after all the city whose colossal temple to Artemis was one of the seven wonders of the ancient world. People travelled throughout the Levant to worship there. The temple generated so much fame and fortune for the city's population, that it nearly cost Paul his life when a silversmith believed his trade was threatened by Pauls' preaching.[23]

Artemis reigned over fertility and childbirth. It is believed that hundreds of eunuch priests, virgin priestesses, and religious prostitutes served her.[24] Typical of the ancient world, worship rituals often involved sexual intercourse. Given the great influence this pagan deity (we would say demon) held over the city's population, the climate of prevailing beliefs would have condoned sexual immorality, rather than condemn it. Nicolaitans may have been the ones spreading those beliefs into the church. If that was indeed the case, they are still alive and active in our own day.

He who has an ear, let him hear what the Spirit says to the churches. To the one who conquers I will grant to eat of the tree of life, which is in the paradise of God.' Revelation 2:7

Having an ear is not the same thing as hearing as every parent knows of their children. Our Father, the ultimate Parent, has had at least six millennia of dealing with His kids. How well He knows that like Gollum in "The Lord of the Rings" we slap our spiritual hands over our ears and say, "I'm not listening" — even when the voice is coming from within us. Ever the optimist, with this announcement the Lord calls for an even wider audience to give an ear. Not just the Ephesian believers, but "the churches"—that includes all of us—are to pay close attention to "what the Spirit says."

Putting it in this way makes us harken back to all the preceding messages as sayings of the Spirit intend for us to hear. This confirms our hunch that these letters contain necessary revelations for our End Times as well as their times. It also points us forward to the promise which follows. "The tree of life" will be granted as food to those who conquer. This is the food we're to seek—not the unholy diet of feeding on the things of the world which the Nicolaitan error represents. Just as we cannot serve God and mammon, we cannot love the world and still have the love of the Father in us.[25] Jesus is the only "tree of life" offered to us! Feeding on Him will enable us to conquer our wayward flesh (by denying Self) and survive a warring world (by clinging to Jesus). Those who conquer by feeding on Jesus down here, will be granted the joy of feeding on Him "in the paradise of God."

CHAPTER 4

THE SECOND CHURCH: SMYRNA

Revelation 2:8-11

How would you like to get a letter saying unavoidable suffering was coming your way? And that the devil himself would be behind it, taking a personal interest in the pain he would be inflicting. You might stop checking the mail after that one! You would probably hope that the sender got it wrong. The trouble is this Sender is Jesus and you know He knows what He's talking about. Oh, you'll check your mail all right—even more frequently now that you know you need every word from "the mouth of God" to survive the coming ordeal.[1] This was Smyrna's predicament. It was also their hope of glory.

Do not fear what you are about to suffer. Behold, the devil is about to throw some of you into prison, that you may be tested, and for ten days you will have tribulation. Be faithful unto death, and I will give you the crown of life. Revelation 2:10

Chief Characteristics

Travelers, commerce and correspondence from Greece or Italy would arrive at Asia Minor's major seaport, Ephesus, then journey up the coast towards Pergamum, before turning east on the interior highway to Laodicea. The letter to the church at Smyrna would have been the second letter delivered.

Now called Izmir and presently the third largest city in Turkey, ancient Smyrna earns the distinction of being truly ancient. Having survived in almost continuous settlement for the last 5,000 years, Smyrna outlived its distant contemporary, Troy of Homer's "Iliad" fame. Being situated close to Greece was an advantage. Alexander the Great re-founded Smyrna after it had lain uninhabited for three hundred years. It quickly recovered its former wealth and prominence. The city Paul would have known from his missionary travels was a thriving commercial center competing with Ephesus and Pergamum to be Rome's foremost city in Asia. Smyrna was celebrated for its wealth, beauty, library, school of medicine, and rhetorical tradition.[2] Nevertheless, the devil used this cultural metropolis as a staging ground for his attack against the church Paul planted. The cultured elites of our day are likely to do the same. Paul's trenchant observation still applies.

For consider your calling, brothers: not many of you were wise according to worldly standards, not many were powerful, not many were of noble birth. 1 Corinthians 1:26

Pre-Figured in Scripture

The Fiery Furnace

These young Israelite men—Shadrach, Meshach, and Abednego—either put us to shame or show us the way to go, depending on how you look at it. While still newly appointed to service in King Nebuchadnezzar's province of Babylon, these faithful Jews quietly refused to bow to his image. For this unpretentious act of faithfulness to their God, Shadrach, Meshach and Abednego were "maliciously accused" by enemies jealous of their access to the king.[3] The indignant king flew into a rage every bit as hot as his famous furnace. Knowing it wouldn't help to appeal to the deranged king—a precursor of the antichrist to come—they cast themselves upon the mercy of heaven.

Apparently, they believed that God could save them, but they didn't know He would. That consideration was beside the point, however. No matter what, they would rather die than take the mark. Sorry, that should have read, "bow to the image." Without the gospel to guide them, with only the Hebrew scriptures to support them, they boldly declared that they had an unshakeable hope of heaven (if all other hope failed). These are true heroes of the faith! Jesus would be asking the same measure of devotion to be displayed by His beloved believers in Smyrna. The same enemy was after them. He was working through different human vessels, but his hatred of the saints remained as red hot as ever. Soon, he will be turning his ire in our direction. His rage is unabated. Our God remains undefeated. Let us be undeterred.

"If this be so, our God whom we serve is able to deliver us from the burning fiery furnace, and he will deliver us out of your hand, O king. But if not, be it known to you, O king, that we will not serve your gods or worship the golden image that you have set up." Daniel 3:17-18

Revealed by Scripture

To the Church in Smyrna

"And to the angel of the church in Smyrna write: 'The words of the first and the last, who died and came to life. Revelation 2:8

This second letter begins with the now familiar address "to the angel of the church" in Smyrna.[4] The words John is being told to write would not be necessary for an angel to read. It's for the believers. The unfallen celestial beings have 20/20 spiritual sight and perfect memories. They neither need to be told nor reminded who Jesus is ("the first and last") or what He has done ("died and came to life"). But we do. We need a lot of encouragement on that score, so difficult it is for us to ascend to those heights of spiritual sight which angels (possibly) take for granted. They see daily—in the unfading light of heaven's eternal day—exactly who sits on the throne and they are in entire agreement with all His decrees.

We need coaxing on that score too. Not every path He wants us to take, not everything He wants us to release seems to hold the promise of life. Jesus is, therefore, providing encouragement for the believers in Smyrna by reminding them—in advance— that the One who will be giving them some bad news about upcoming events, is the Author of the gospel's good news. They (and we) will be asked to walk into an uncertain, forbidding future, but the One leading the way has already proven His power to conquer death with life. He knows how all this will work out in the end, because neither end nor beginning are beyond His knowing: He is Himself "the first and the last"—the "Author and Finisher" of our race.[5]

"'I know your tribulation and your poverty (but you are rich) and the slander of those who say that they are Jews and are not, but are a synagogue of Satan. Revelation 2:9

Jesus sees with compassion their embattled condition. "Tribulation" means trouble, but of a special kind that usually has persecution added to it. Poverty, for instance, would be struggle enough for the average person's faith and life, but these believers must also contend with the sting of "slander"—of unjustified accusations hurled against them. The troublemakers "say" they are of Jewish descent and belief (these typically are one and the same), but Jesus sees them differently. The synagogue where they gather to worship does not center around Him, but the evil one. Theirs is a "synagogue of Satan."

We have all been forewarned by Jesus that a day is coming when even those who kill us will believe they are doing God a favor.[6] For the Smyrna believers that day is rapidly approaching, though at the moment perhaps all they have contended with is expulsion from the synagogue. Such "excommunication" and the accompanying "anathemas" (formal curses) became a common way of making Jewish Christians feel blamed for the temple's destruction two decades earlier. After all, it was the Christians' leader who (they may have alleged) brought the curse by prophesying the disaster.

That Jesus sees us differently than our detractors is cause for celebration. There is "no condemnation" for those who are in Christ Jesus.[7] Not only that, but He will allow no tongue raised against us to prosper.[8] So, the position of these believers is secure. In fact, it is far better than they believe it to be. That's because the other side of this coin is that Jesus also sees us differently than we see ourselves. The Smyrna Christians thought of themselves as poor—and may have "slandered" themselves and their God by saying so. Not so, dear saints!

Jesus says, "but you are rich." It's a gentle (parenthetical) reminder that they won the spiritual lottery when He popped the question and they said, "Yes." They (as we) are inheritors of the boundless, "unsearchable riches of Christ."[9] Never think for one moment that your spiritual pockets are empty!

Do not fear what you are about to suffer. Behold, the devil is about to throw some of you into prison, that you may be tested, and for ten days you will have tribulation. Be faithful unto death, and I will give you the crown of life. Revelation 2:10

Now comes the unwanted news. Perhaps they were already reading the writing on the wall and hoping it could be erased. Persecution of this magnitude doesn't grow in a vacuum. Telltale signs like squishy spots of mold on a rotting wall betray the vile thing growing beneath the surface. What they fear is about to happen. They will indeed "suffer." Some will be thrown "into prison." Others will need to be "faithful unto death." As a church they will all fall into the hands of "the devil" himself, but they do not have to fall into fear. Why? Those who are faithful will be given "the crown of life."

Here is a threefold source of confidence. First, Jesus knows what is coming. Nothing takes Him by surprise. He already has counter measures in place. Second, He set limits to it— "ten days." This doesn't tell us how long, nor would it have them. It isn't a secret code we're meant to crack, but a word to keep them from breaking under pressure: The time is fixed and relatively brief. Hang on! By Paul's own letters they would know that Jesus won't let them "be tested" beyond their ability (in Him) to bear it.[10] Finally, Jesus will make sure that the reward outweighs the pain of the passage.[11] Not just this trial, but the "crown of life" is also set before them.

Some say that there are five crowns in heaven waiting for believers to receive.[12] There is no need to investigate them here, only to know that they are there. This tells us that our Lord knows how to reward faithfulness. His own love of loyalty is such that He prizes it when He sees it showing up in us. Perhaps you're thinking you don't need a crown. A Mercedes-

Benzes maybe (a la Janis Joplin) or not even that. Anyway, who needs a crown? When would you wear it? Just let the Lord decide that one. Don't you love the image of those twenty-four elders in heaven casting down their crowns before the Lamb?[13] Now that's the way to give praise! It is such a beautiful witness to His worth. Well, how could they do that if they didn't have crowns? They are promised to us, too, if—the big IF—we are faithful.

He who has an ear, let him hear what the Spirit says to the churches. The one who conquers will not be hurt by the second death.' Revelation 2:11

For a second time in this book, we are asked to use our ears to hear. After the somewhat bleak forecast for the future they (we) just received, we need to hear with the kind of listening that grows faith. "Faith comes by hearing" and hearing comes by the Word of God which brings the gospel—the "word of Christ"—home to our hearts.[14] Only faith rising in the heart has strength to help us persevere. Only trust that flows from faith in a river of peace has the power to crush our enemies beneath our feet.[15] Faith first, then faithfulness can readily follow. Reverse the order and it's a grueling, uphill battle usually ending in a defeated, downhill slide. Jesus is speaking words of faith to enkindle faith so that won't happen. Not for these believers. Not for us either.

The "second death"—the lake of fire—will never be known to us. It is reserved for those who refused to die to self in this life, those who rejected the way of faith and grace. The first death is the one we all pass through, for "it is appointed to men once to die, but after this the judgment."[16] When judgment comes at the Great White Throne, there will be no remedy for those who were not found faithful in this life. Then, it will be too late. Until then, while there is still breath within us, it is always possible to repent, get faith and become faithful.

CHAPTER 5

THE THIRD CHURCH: PERGAMUM

Revelation 2:12-17

What do you do when the world's depravity is weaponized against you? What if you're living in the very heart of the Enemy's empire? How do you handle it when you have to pass Satan's throne on your way to work? Sound extreme? This was daily life for the believers who dwelt where Satan reigned. If you can't run from such a place, you run to Jesus to keep you safe. Jesus calls on the Pergamum church to do just that—stick close. Hold fast, listen well and repent so that they can conquer this extreme situation. It's good advice for us, too.

"'I know where you dwell, where Satan's throne is." Revelation 2:13a

Chief Characteristics

Travelers, commerce and correspondence from Greece or Italy would arrive at Asia Minor's major seaport, Ephesus, then journey up the coast towards Pergamum, before turning east on the interior highway to Laodicea. The letter to the church at Pergamum would have been the third letter delivered.

Though Pergamum was seen by the Lord to be the place where Satan had his throne, no pagan citizen would have seen it that way. Their civic pride would have been through the roof. Pergamum had been one of the most beautiful and prestigious cities in Asia Minor during the Greek period. It competed with Ephesus for being the province's first city under Roman rule. Her architecture, however, knew no rivals. Treasures of art adorned her public buildings. Unparalleled city planning filled her squares with gymnasium, temples, a theater, a racetrack, a library and oh, by the way, the Altar of Zeus, Satan's throne.[1]

Pre-Figured in Scripture

Righteous Lot: Surviving in Sodom

Lot gives us an Old Testament portrayal of someone who dwelt where Satan reigned. The Enemy's hold over Sodom and Gomorrah was so complete that the cities had to be destroyed. Depravity reached a point where redemption became impossible. Get ready: This will happen around us in the days to come. As it does, we'll understand Lot's predicament. We've heard the story of how Abraham interceded for the wicked city, how the Lord rescued Lot and his family at the last minute, and how the fire from heaven fell in judgment. That's not the whole story.

Peter gives us insight into the part we don't usually see. He shows us the distress that the wickedness around Lot caused that righteous man to suffer. Without a doubt, depravity brings punishing consequences upon those who pursue it, but it also has a "tormenting" effect upon those who live within sight and sound. Pure hearts grieve for those who grieve God—not wishing any to be so lost. They also cringe in horror over the devil's incarnation in human flesh and blood and the appalling things he "inspires" them to do. This part of Lot's experience will come our way, too. As much as we may not want to think about these things, it helps to prepare our hearts in advance in case they show do up.

And if he rescued righteous Lot, greatly distressed by the sensual conduct of the wicked (for as that righteous man lived among them day after day, he was tormenting his righteous soul over their lawless deeds that he saw and heard); then the Lord knows how to rescue the godly from trials. 2 Peter 2:7-9

Revealed by Scripture

To the Church in Pergamum

"And to the angel of the church in Pergamum write: 'The words of him who has the sharp two-edged sword. Revelation 2:12

Jesus begins the letter in His customary way with an address "to the angel" of the church in Pergamum.[2] Since the message of this letter (as with the others) is clearly directed to the people of the church, the opening words strike a familiar cord heard in the formal speeches of our day. Our best speakers typically give honor to the principle dignitaries present, before taking up the real theme they are bringing to the larger audience. By including the angel in this address Jesus accomplishes a dual purpose: He gives honor to the angelic dignitary (something Peter also advises us to do)[3] and makes the church aware that they have one watching over them at the same time. We all tend to behave better if someone we respect is watching. Knowing that Jesus sees all we do should be enough both to keep us in line and to keep us feeling secure. "But He's in heaven!" may be the thought in the back of our mind. In that case church, let it be known that there is an angel in the house!

Our divine and heavenly Watcher is not sitting on His Hands fretting over the state of His poor, beleaguered church unable to affect events. No, He has a sword ready to Hand and not just any sword, but "a sharp two-edged sword." To understand the image in the context of its historic setting, we should recall that early swords of bronze and iron could not hold a sharp edge as more modern techniques later allowed. For that reason alone, a two-edged sword proved its worth on ancient battlefields for once the first edge grew dull, a second sharp edge remained. Jesus is not only saying that His sword is sharp, but that it stays sharp.

From other texts of scripture, we understand that a sword represents the authority that even our own governments have for keeping the peaceful reign of law within their borders and keeping unlawful invaders out. Paul wrote that our rulers do not "bear the sword in vain" but know how to carry out "God's wrath on the wrongdoer."[4] Jesus is about to warn some in the church against compromise with certain notorious wrongdoers of their day. He does not hold the sword in vain either.

These letters offer yet another example of the sword He wields. His very words are "sharper than any two-edged sword, piercing to the division of soul and of spirit, of joints and of marrow, and discerning the thoughts and intentions of the heart."[5] Who among us has not known what it is like to have our secret thoughts instantly exposed and overturned by the entry of His word? We need Him to cut through the foolishness of our thinking and get us back on track with His wisdom. It's a great good thing for us that His sword stays sharp.

"'I know where you dwell, where Satan's throne is. Revelation 2:13a

In studying scripture, a key guiding principle is "context is king." This little verse proves it in a powerful way. First, we see Jesus saying He knows their context. They "dwell" in a territory that lies under the enemy's power and influence. They are living in a spiritual battle zone and their Lord knows what they are up against. For them the challenge to be faithful with be vexed by powerful temptations; their daily life will be assaulted beyond what other believers face. He knows our context too. He knows everything in our past that makes it so hard to be faithful in the present. He completely understands. And just as with these Pergamum believers, He is present to help us dwell in safety by His side.

The Pergamum believer's special challenge is that they dwell "where Satan's throne is." Evidently, the enemy laid claim to the area of Pergamum in such a way that it became the center of his power, the very seat—the throne—of his reign in that part of the world. For the last two thousand years of biblical study, this would likely have seemed an esoteric reference to a by-gone era. There are no thrones, no temples dedicated to the pagan deities in the Middle East. Almost all those shrines were destroyed when Christianity first conquered the Mediterranean area. It is indeed true that Satan is still the "god of this world" who blinds the minds of unbelievers.[6] We also understand from Paul that as "Prince of the Power of the Air" he rules over the world from "heavenly places."[7] But surely his throne in ancient Turkey is a thing of the past.

The pagan worship of Asia Minor (present day Turkey) was centered in Pergamum.[8] The throne of Satan that Jesus referred to would have been the city's monumental altar dedicated to Zeus, the most powerful god of the Roman world. The evil one's pride is such that he would have occupied the highest seat of worship, hence his "throne" was visibly present in those days. Of course, the people would not have known it was Satan they were worshipping any more than they would have realized they "fellowshipped" with demons when they bowed before their idols.[9] Jesus knew. Through Him—through the sword of His Word—we also know. All these invisible layers of deception are pieced through and the enemy is unmasked. Satan was hiding in plain sight! When the fire of Christian faith burned through these lands, the ancient gods were exposed as frauds and abandoned as deities. Their empty temples were neglected or destroyed, literally covered by the shifting sands of time. If only the story could have ended there!

The great thing about the past in the Mediterranean Basin is that you can dig it up. The past is so rich and so thoroughly scattered about that practically any stone you kick in modern Turkey (for instance) may have fallen from a ruin or will strike one before it stops. So, it happened that when a German engineer, Carl Humann, began excavating the old city in 1864, he unearthed the massive Altar of Zeus, previously lost to history. No one knew it was there. No one that is except our Lord and His arch Enemy. From Turkey the historic "treasure" was taken stone by stone to Berlin and housed on the city's Museum Island where it stands to this day.

When the Pergamum museum opened to the public in 1930, the Altar caught the attention of Adolph Hitler and his chief architect, Albert Speer. When called upon by his Chancellor to design an imposing stage platform for the upcoming Nuremburg rallies, Speer turned to the throne of Satan for inspiration. The six mass rallies held there from 1933-1938 proved critical for the rise of National Socialism as a quasi-religious ideology which captured the hearts and minds of so many of the German people. The Nazi party went from being a gang of thugs and political extremists to a national movement which carried a galvanized and united country into world war. Once again, Satan occupied his throne during those terrible years of "blood and iron."[10]

The Altar of Zeus still stands within the Pergamum Museum in Berlin. It should be noted that two prophets with long-standing track records of holy living and accurate words, say that they have been informed by the Lord through divine visitations that the antichrist will use Berlin as his political center of influence. One is Sundar Selvaraj Sadhu. The other is Neville Johnson. Search for them on the internet. If you believe they may have a true word, pray for Berlin, for Germany and for the church that "dwells" there.

Yet you hold fast my name, and you did not deny my faith even in the days of Antipas my faithful witness, who was killed among you, where Satan dwells. Revelation 2:13b

This is a wonderful word of praise. Despite the oppressive context of their location, the believers of Pergamum still "hold fast." They remained faithful to the Lord of heaven against efforts by the god of this world to get them to "deny" the faith. The darkest time of persecution they passed through so far happened "in the days of Antipas," who was martyred for being a "faithful witness." This killing is directly linked by Jesus to the working of Satan, since this is the location where he "dwells." Since the days of Job, the evil one is known for going "to and fro upon the earth."[11] Pergamum is where he pitched his tent.

Interesting, the Lord says that it is "His faith" that the Christians did not deny. We usually think of it as "our faith" or as faith that is given to us because we fell into doubt and unbelief and required the gospel to help us recover the faith we need. Our faith is in Jesus, or in God, or in the scriptures, but this is different. It is the faith *of* Jesus, the faith that Jesus relies upon. His faith. It's not faith in Himself. As God He has no need of anyone, no need for faith. It would be as the "son of man" that Jesus needed faith. In fact, we see Him exercising faith everywhere in the gospels, but in one place it shines brightest. Where? In the Garden of Gethsemane. In His moment of greatest trial, our human representative looked up to the Father and yielded in entire faith-surrender to whatever was required. That's the faith of Jesus and it's the faith He commends the Pergamum believers for having during their time of excruciating trial.

But I have a few things against you: you have some there who hold the teaching of Balaam, who taught Balak to put a stumbling block before the sons of Israel, so that they might eat food sacrificed to idols and practice sexual immorality. Revelation 2:14

Unfortunately, though their faith held steadfast, their walk was not without stumbling. Jesus says He has "a few things" against them. This indicates that there will be more than one, but also hints that they aren't big problems yet, when compared to the big thing he had just praised them for—their faithful grip on His faith. If we don't let go His Hand, He can pull us through. He holds those who hold on to Him. That's the paradox of faith and faithfulness.

Though that paradox may hold mysteries for us, there's no mystery here about the problem Jesus wants resolved. This is one that has a long history with God's people, going back to the wilderness—sexual compromise. Then, the renegade prophet Balaam was enlisted by the pagan king Balak to curse the Israelites. That he could not do. He held firm against the bribes saying he could not curse what God blessed. Nevertheless, he gave treacherous counsel to Balak that God would bring a curse on His own people if the Moabites could entice them into sexual sin.[12] Upon being invited to their festivals, the Israelites compromised sexually and ate food sacrificed to the Moabite gods.[13] One sin led to the other. Then came the plague that killed 24,000 before it was finally averted. This is what earned Balaam his unique place of infamy in the biblical record.

For the Lord to name the ideas going around the church as "the teaching of Balaam" is therefore to expose them as false and castigate them as thoroughly wicked. The judgment upon the sins that Balaam's counsel inspired was swift and deadly. It is not the Heart of our Lord to be other than compassionate, merciful and slow to anger—qualities He revealed to Moses at Sinai before setting out on the journey which led to Moab.[14] He doesn't want to bring judgment to the Pergamum believers, but He will have to if they keep going in this wrong direction.

So also you have some who hold the teaching of the Nicolaitans. Revelation 2:15

The other "thing" that needed correction is the "teaching of the Nicolaitans." This is the very thing He brought as a charge against the church of Ephesus. False teaching in the Church acts like a disease and can spread as easily. Many germs are airborne. They spread from mouth to mouth, as one coughs and the other breathes. False teachings spread from mouth to ear, as one speaks and the other listens. Jesus would have this church stop listening. What it was that they were hearing is a thing lost to time. For speculation, see the previous passage about the church in Ephesus. For now, it is enough to know that Jesus may deal with us about more than one thing at a time. Even so, it is never His intention to overwhelm us—that He could easily do—but to liberate us.[15]

Therefore repent. If not, I will come to you soon and war against them with the sword of my mouth. Revelation 2:16

Having made plain the danger, the hoped-for response is now given: "therefore repent." Repentance is always the way of escape. Turn from the wrong thing to the right thing. Turn from sin to the living God. It sounds so simple in theory and it works so well in practice. Why don't we repent immediately? The answer could lie here in the way Jesus speaks to motivate them. The lie of the wrong way is that it can go on forever and that there will be no negative consequences. Jesus slices through both those fabrications. First, He will come "soon"—this party's not going to last. Second, He Himself will "war" against them if they don't repent. Who would want the Lord for an adversary? He uses the sword of His words to warn them that the "sword of my mouth" is coming. Indeed, it is. We will see this scene unfold dramatically towards the end of the book.

He who has an ear, let him hear what the Spirit says to the churches. To the one who conquers I will give some of the hidden manna, and I will give him a white stone, with a new name written on the stone that no one knows except the one who receives it.' Revelation 2:17

The Lord wants us all to listen well. He desires no one to be lost, or to have to experience the difficulty of His dealings. If these believers hold fast (as they have under other trials) and if they keep repenting (as this time of temptation requires), they will arrive victorious on the other side of the struggle. Therefore, to become "one who conquers" means we will have to learn to listen well. To such a one three things are promised: manna, a stone and a name.

The manna is "hidden manna" indicating that we will never find it by looking for it. Only by looking to Him in faithful obedience, will we be led to feed upon it. Believers undergoing persecution such as Pergamum experienced would need supernatural measures of provision to keep them going which is what the manna represents. The Church of our day may soon be going under darkened days of persecution worldwide. We may also need the Lord's release of hidden manna. There is nothing we can do to prevent persecution from coming. However, there is much we can do for the manna to be revealed. We can look to Him, listen well, repent often and the promised manna will appear.

We are promised also a "white stone" with a "new name" written upon it. In ancient times a white stone would be cast to render a favorable verdict. Jesus cast His vote in our favor when He declared us "Not guilty!" through faith in His Blood. The stone speaks of the unchangeable nature of that verdict. The name indicates that what this divine restoration will bring home is nothing less than a brand-new identity in Him. Indeed, we are already new creations with old things passing away.[16]

Even now, our new life—our true life—is a mystery "hid with Christ in God."[17] John, this John, wrote in his first letter that "what we will be has not yet appeared; but we know that when he appears we shall be like him, because we shall see him as he is."[18] Is Jesus promising here that if we keep our eyes on Him, if we listen with a heart to repent and obey, that He will bring forth the person we already are deep inside? We don't even know yet who that person really is. The mystery unfolds only as we "conquer" each new challenge clinging to His life and leadership.

CHAPTER 6

THE FOURTH CHURCH: THYATIRA
Revelation 2:18-29

Tolerance is a lovely virtue when it is exercised to allow the full variety of God-given life to grow with freedom. It has its place, but it also has its limits. God gives all manner of personalities and gifts to people, but He never gives sin. The Thyratiran believers thought that they were giving grace to a questionable prophetess in their community, but in Jesus' eyes they were "tolerating" her sin. That put fire in His eyes! This letter begins as a wake-up call to a church drifting from its moral moorings. Then, Jesus opens the letter and speaks directly through it to us. We need to hear what He's saying here just as much as they did.

But I have this against you, that you tolerate that woman Jezebel, who calls herself a prophetess and is teaching and seducing my servants. Revelation 2:20

Chief Characteristics

Travelers, commerce and correspondence from Greece or Italy would arrive at Asia Minor's major seaport, Ephesus, then journey up the coast towards Pergamum, before turning east on the interior highway to Laodicea. The letter to the church at Thyatira would have been the fourth letter delivered.

The ancient town of Thyatira never reached the size or stature of its neighbors Ephesus, Pergamum and Smyrna. It was situated within the kingdom of Pergamum on the Roman road that led to Laodicea. Despite being of relative unimportance to the world, it was still territory coveted by the Enemy. He sent in one of his most notorious temptresses to lead the church astray. Apparently, some were letting down their guard and giving way to her charms. In view of this, the city's position "on the road to" Laodicea poetically describes the direction these believers were headed, since Laodicea's church is synonymous with complete moral and spiritual laxity. Jesus wrote to stop their stumble before it became their downfall.

Pre-Figured in Scripture

Delilah: The Temptress of Samson

The Jezebel of Israel's history is infamous for the way she incited King Ahab to "do evil in the sight of the Lord."[1] She promoted idolatry, persecuted the faithful and pursued the prophet Elijah, driving him from the country. She embodied the treacherous, manipulative ways of her namesake spirit. The false religion she brought to the Northern Kingdom did indeed encourage ritual sex and cultic prostitution, though she herself is not known for sexual immorality. She seemed to have been faithful to Ahab to a fault, going beyond the law to satisfy his desires.

Delilah, on the other hand, has a name that cannot be disassociated from sexual scandal. She sizzled on the outside, schemed on the inside. Samson fell for her, traded his inheritance as a Nazarite to bed her, and lost his divine strength because of her. She's the temptress that prefigures the Jezebel of this letter, whose sexual immorality drew the notice and harsh discipline of the Lord. Sadly, Samson's Delilah is never said to have loved him, though the text says he loved her. She was a deceiver who used her charms to bring down the Philistine's greatest enemy. Thyatira's Jezebel used her charms in a vain attempt to bring down her master's greatest enemy, the church in her region. Unlike Samson with Delilah, Jesus saw Jezebel's heart and rejected her. He wants us to do the same.

She made him sleep on her knees. And she called a man and had him shave off the seven locks of his head. Then she began to torment him, and his strength left him. Judges 16:19

Revealed by Scripture

To the Church in Thyatira

"And to the angel of the church in Thyatira write: 'The words of the Son of God, who has eyes like a flame of fire, and whose feet are like burnished bronze. Revelation 2:18

Look out denizens of Thyatira! The Son of God has fire in His eyes and He's looking right at you! Would it not startle you, if the letter in your hand caught fire as you read it? Something like that seems intended by the way Jesus begins this letter. Of course, it opens with the familiar greeting to the "angel of the church" but by now we all know it is the people of the church He has in mind.[2] What He has on His mind—as with us who bear His Image—shows up in the look of His eyes. Since they can't see Him, He lets them know up front that He "has eyes like a flame of fire."

It's true He used these same phrases by way of general introduction to John while first appearing to Him on Patmos. That was before this series of individual church letter began. The opening parts of that earlier description seem tailor-made to fit the context of each church He addresses. The companion part of this description includes the sight of His feet that "are like burnished bronze." Burnished bronze in antiquity epitomized the best metal they could produce with its great strength and dazzling beauty, as sunlight or torches played off the highly polished surface. Forming such a metal and forging it required the blazing heat of a refiner's furnace. The fire in our Lord's eyes is matched by the fiery trial He walked through to forge the path of our return. In a moment, He will call for them to return.

"'I know your works, your love and faith and service and patient endurance, and that your latter works exceed the first." Revelation 2:19

Jesus praises them for four "works" —not virtues. Virtues are what flow from us. They disclose our true nature wherever it has been fused with His. Works, on the other hand, are virtuous activities. This is not a full compliment. Nevertheless, although they are having to "work" at it, they are succeeding in the area of love, faith and patient endurance. This measure of progress earns words here of praise and approval. Perfection is our unattainable goal. We are to be perfect as our Heavenly Father is perfect, but please catch the wink: We can only do our best with His help. We can only be our best, if we die to self so that Jesus can live through us. That will only happen fully and finally when we arrive in heaven. Until then, there is (thank God) measurable progress that can be made walking with Him in the right direction.

Progress, however, means that there is always room for improvement. Jesus compliments them for their work of "love," the highest of the virtues; for their "faith" which works through love; for their "service" which is love's most tangible expression; and finally, for their "patient endurance" which spreads love's inward kindness to others—when the pressure is on. So far so good. In fact, it seems very good. Then, comes the first hint that all is not well in Thyatira land. When we remember that love is the foremost virtue and that first among the many loves is loving devotion to the One who loves us, then we will catch the wind of what's coming. Jesus now tells them that their "latter works exceed the first." That's not the divinely preferred order!

But I have this against you, that you tolerate that woman Jezebel, who calls herself a prophetess and is teaching and seducing my servants to practice sexual immorality and to eat food sacrificed to idols Revelation 2:20

Without counting the words, this certainly feels like the shortest preamble to the "punch" that the Lord has taken so far. One all-too-brief sentence of encouragement, then it's straight to point of correction. Combined with His fiery look, this alerts us (and them) that this warning is urgent. We don't say to a child about to step in front of traffic, "You know, I really liked the way you handled yourself back there in the classroom. I'm a friend of your father, but I need to tell you…" No! We shout first and introduce ourselves later. Jesus is practically shouting. That woman Jezebel would get anyone's goat. Not His of course—He doesn't have a goat nature the devil could get a rise from. But the Thyratirans do. The problem is rather than getting vexed with her, they're getting along with her.

Jesus faults them for their "tolerance." Oh, what does that say about our "politically correct" ways? We bend over backwards trying to keep everyone from feeling disparaged or worse, excluded. Intolerance is practically the only "sin" left in our modern world—or at least the only one a person can safely express intolerance towards. Jesus doesn't want "that woman" tolerated. Her rap sheet is long. She "calls herself" by a title and thereby claims a position in His Body that He never gave her. She's no "prophetess" though honorable women prophets abound in scripture. This real-life imposter proves her colors by "teaching and seducing" others.

That her teachings are false is evident by what she promotes: "sexual immorality" and eating "food sacrificed to idols." Whether Jezebel's "seducing" is by her beguiling way of spreading these false teachings, or by direct allurement is not clear. What is clear is that this is now a consistent theme running through the first three letters. We need to be sure it's not running through our life or that of our church. It is also starkly clear that Jesus doesn't tolerate sexual immorality or trafficking with false idols in any way, shape or form. His patience is not a sign of tolerance. His silence cannot be taken as approval. These sins—and helping people get free of them— should be as serious a thing to us as it is to Him.

I gave her time to repent, but she refuses to repent of her sexual immorality. Revelation 2: 21

Now, we see how the Lord has been working behind the scenes. Yes, He was sitting back. Yes, He was being silent. No, He was not abandoning the cause. Grace, in one way of viewing it, is God giving us time to turn around. Even as He gives us time, He gives us signs. He speaks in the heart the warning words, "You know this isn't right." One way or the other they are there. He also frustrates our path and plans. The obstacles are meant to wake us up like those bump strips they put on country highways just before the stop sign appears. He has been providing this gracious service for Jezebel. Let's don't forget that He has also been trying to issue warnings to her through other church members. That's His charge against them. Rather than reprimanding her, they are allowing her to operate freely. All in the name of tolerance. Sound familiar?

By the way, why would any mother name their child Jezebel? Why would any believer not change that name on conversion? Perhaps, in some mysterious way she is secretly living up to the name. We would say she's chosen to own it. Apparently, she is fulfilling her name without apology. "She refuses" to change her ways which is the essence of rebellion. Day after day it's always the same game with her. She is playing at church, promoting herself as a guide to others, but refusing to be led by her church's true Prophet and Teacher. Has she no idea that the Lord put a stop sign on her path? Can't she feel the wake-up bumps? Evidently not.

22 Behold, I will throw her onto a sickbed, and those who commit adultery with her I will throw into great tribulation, unless they repent of her works, 23 and I will strike her children dead. And all the churches will know that I am he who searches mind and heart, and I will give to each of you according to your works. Revelation 2:22-23

Reading Leviticus 26, one sees how the Lord spelled out in advance to the Israelites the chastisements they would increasingly suffer, if they ever fell away from trusting and obeying Him. He knew they would! He knew in advance that they would fail to repent no matter how He worked with them. He forewarned their future exile. It became unavoidable. Merely because He foresees our fall, doesn't mean He desires it or wills it or needs it. That He can foresee our stubborn resistance to His grace and still work with us to the bitter end is a marvel to behold. We see Him working here with Jezebel. Will she repent? We don't know, but it doesn't look promising for her or for "those who commit adultery with her."

One bright spot is that at least her flaming disaster might light the way for others to avoid her end. What sane person, however, would want their life to become only a negative example? The book of each person's life while they are living may be a confusing lesson to read, but in the end we will all point only one way or the other. Jesus states two truths which He sees as lessons we can learn from Jezebel and His dealings with her. First, He "searches" then He "gives." Jesus searches everyone. He is not casually observing our behavior, much less monitoring us only occasionally from the distance. He intentionally probes us to the depths of thought and feeling, motive and desire. Not even our slightest flaw is hidden from His jeweler's eye. This is going on 24/7!

Jezebel thought she could get away with pulling the wool over her fellow church-goers' eyes. Jesus saw through it all and though He waited, giving her time to repent, He would act decisively when the time comes. As they say, "What goes around, comes around." That's because we have not just a Savior who will forgive our sins, but a Lord who will bring us to account if we refuse to repent of them. That day of reckoning is coming for Jezebel, but the warning in this verse isn't only for her. It's for us: "I will give to each of you according to your works." That's Jesus shifting the focus of the passage from "that woman"—the notorious Jezebel of legendary wickedness—to the other sin-prone souls He keeps an eye on. That would be everyone else who ever lived. Feel "included" yet? Good. Political correctness is dying on the vine.

24 But to the rest of you in Thyatira, who do not hold this teaching, who have not learned what some call the deep things of Satan, to you I say, I do not lay on you any other burden. 25 Only hold fast what you have until I come. Revelation 2:24-25

Fortunately, "the rest" of the believers in Thyatira did not "hold this teaching." They discerned correctly that what Jezebel promoted was not of God and avoided it like the plague. They had the scriptures which are entirely clear on these key issues, but such is the power of the deceiver that truth can be turned inside out. That Jezebel was good at deception is shown by how far this infection spread and by the serious steps the Lord took to remedy it. Was she also deceived? Was she an unwitting victim herself, or did she know full-well that she was serving Satan, rather than Jesus? This is a hard question to answer from the outside looking in. It would require soul-searching honesty on the part of the one deceived and a willingness to be utterly transparent with others about it. That's something the true deceiver keeps his victims from doing at all costs.

It does seem from this context that Jezebel had to be in on the deception. Jesus didn't say that she was the one promoting "what some call the deep things of Satan," but she is likely at the source of it. The power of prophetic vision and artful teaching is that other believers, who may not have those gifts, begin thinking that perhaps this person knows "deep" things. It requires a solid knowledge of scripture with the wisdom to discern spirits both of people and of the invisible realm in order to unmask the deceiver. This problem is amplified if the person has a personal charisma, a ready command of scripture and an elevated status in the church.

Just what this teaching consisted of is anybody's guess at this point. Like so much else it is lost to time. Beyond that it is a true enigma. Deceptive teaching normally stays clear of any association with Satan for obvious reasons. Usually only Satanists practicing their craft outside of the church would want to go deep and long on his things—and boast about it by naming it. This is where it may help to remember that Satan has another side, so to speak—that of Lucifer, the "light bringer."

Many who pursue occult knowledge believe that Lucifer is humanity's friend, since it was the "evil" Yahweh who wanted to keep knowledge away from us in Eden. Lucifer, on the other hand, set humanity free to pursue (his) knowledge and wisdom. You get the drift. It is easy to see how this kind of thinking could turn any idea in the Bible inside out. Still, we don't know, nor do we need to. That's not God keeping us in the dark—He just didn't write His Book to satisfy every point of human curiosity. But He did put what we needed in it—to keep us from the dark!

26 The one who conquers and who keeps my works until the end, to him I will give authority over the nations, 27 and he will rule them with a rod of iron, as when earthen pots are broken in pieces, even as I myself have received authority from my Father. 28 And I will give him the morning star. Revelation 2:26-28

We saw in the previous letter that for us to "conquer" will require listening, repenting, obeying and holding fast. The promise here is that for those who pursue the way of faith and "keep my works to the end" a great measure of authority will be granted. We'll look into that promise in a moment. For now, there is a mystery to probe. It is strange, is it not, that Jesus tells us (for He shifted the focus to all of us in verse 23) that we are to keep "His works"? Not keep "our works" heading in the right direction, as He previously praised this group of believers for doing (verse 19). Somehow our work has become keeping His work. See the shift?

What does Jesus mean by keeping His works? One "work" might lead our thinking to the cross, His great, one of a kind work of redemption, but that's not what He said. Perhaps, however, by "works" He is pointing us towards keeping the works He directly assigns us to do under His leadership. Those are His works, growing out of His plans, not ours. That would almost fit the bill. Yet, another way to understand the riddle, however, is to do the works that He did while He walked among us. Of those works, two especially leap to mind: miracles and dying to self.

Jesus said to the disciples on their final night together that a day would come when we would do "the works I do; and greater works than these."[3] Those greater works are coming! The glory of this "latter house" of His Body on earth will exceed the supernatural activity of the Early Church.[4] So, say many prophetic voices—and many hearts. For those greater works to come, an even greater work may be required of us. Later that same evening, Jesus knelt alone in the Garden of Gethsemane to do it. The challenge of our times may call for the same level of surrender He reached in the face of the suffering that awaited Him. He worked at it so hard that sweat "like great drops of blood" fell to the ground beneath His knees.[5] Yielding to the Lord without giving way in fear or favor to others is what Jesus wanted from the Thyatirans. He will desire no less from us upon whom the End of the Age is falling.

Assuming we conquer in life and bear up under the weight of these works, we are promised to become "more than conquerors."[6] First given by Paul in the magnificent eighth chapter of Romans, that phrase is explained by Jesus here. Once conquerors gain victory, they become rulers. That's the something "more" which is promised to us. Jesus assures His faithful Bride that we won't be passing around laurel wreaths in heaven, we'll be "given authority" to reign with Him on earth. Not everyone will receive this. Only those who fully submit to His authority now in the ways He just decreed, will be rewarded with ruling over nations then.

To rule with "a rod of iron" necessarily requires being trained by one. A rod in the wrong hand can easily smash an earthen pot "to pieces." Only a well-trained disciple can bring brokenness to peace—to the restoration Jesus desires. As He fully submitted to the Father, so too those who fully submit to Him will share in the authority the Father gave Him for reward. That will usher in the dawning of a new day, the unending Day of Jesus' reign on earth, symbolized by the gift of the "morning star"—the heaven's first sign that a new day has arrived.

He who has an ear, let him hear what the Spirit says to the churches.' Revelation 2:29

Listen, dear heart. Listen. But listen with your heart. "What the Spirit says to the churches" is not a matter of mere words and intellectual understanding. We will need that of course. Nevertheless, as with our own discourse and disclosures, so much more than what is being said is revealed by the way it is said. An unexpected look in the eye, a certain tone of voice, a pause or an inflection are among the many ways we discern what a person—even one we know well—is trying to communicate. Jesus has His own inimitable way of expressing Himself. Some of those ways are recognized by all who listen. Some are unique to each one. The better we know Him, the better we can recognize His voice, the way of His words and the meaning of His ultimate Word, Holy Scripture.

CHAPTER 7

THE FIFTH CHURCH: SARDIS

Revelation 3:1-6

Sometimes the harder you try the "behinder" you get. People pleasing is like that. No matter how hard you try, it's never good enough to keep everybody happy with you. Trying to please God works the same way. The believers of Sardis aren't "ripping and running" with the world (as sinners in the Southern USA describe a lifestyle of immorality). No, these are good church people trying to do good. In fact, they are working so hard at it that it's killing them. If that sounds like anyone you know, read on. Jesus says their works are dead. He sure doesn't sound pleased.

"And to the angel of the church in Sardis write: 'The words of him who has the seven spirits of God and the seven stars. "'I know your works. You have the reputation of being alive, but you are dead. Revelation 3:1

Chief Characteristics

Travelers, commerce and correspondence from Greece or Italy would arrive at Asia Minor's major seaport, Ephesus, then journey up the coast towards Pergamum, before turning east on the interior highway to Laodicea. The letter to the church at Sardis would have been the fifth letter delivered.

Sardis lay on the road to Laodicea from the coast between Thyatira and Philadelphia. Seven centuries prior to the time of these letters, Sardis was capital of the Lydian kingdom and prospered accordingly. The wealth of the last king of Lydia, Croesus, became the stuff of legends. Gold and silver coins were first minted there.[1] It continued as a metropolitan capital under Roman rule. Destroyed by an earthquake in 17 A.D., the city regrouped and rebuilt, recovering its prestige, influence and wealth. These people were hard workers! Ironically, Jesus faulted the believers of Sardis for working hard at the wrong things and hardly working on the right ones.

Pre-Figured in Scripture

The Guest with No Garment

When our incredible Lord walked the earth, He spoke to the people of His day according to their needs. He also launched those same words of life onto a river of time which would carry them safely to our shores. He took the advice He'd given Solomon and cast His bread upon the waters.[2] In our day they are coming back to Him—with us attached. When you put your "End Times glasses" on, it is amazing how much of the Bible comes into focus around the Last Days.

This parable of the wedding feast is an obvious example of a story that had plenty of good lessons in it for those days, but its setting is ours. It's about a feast planned by a king for his son's upcoming marriage. Sound familiar? The marriage supper of the Lamb is just around the corner. The wedding guests are being invited right before our eyes. He will soon be emptying the hedgerows by the greatest harvest the world has ever seen. What joy we'll share in that festal gathering!

We should take care, however, to make sure we're clothed with the proper attire. One of the guests crashed the party. Oh, he accepted the invitation and came, but something went terribly wrong. He neglected to put on the "wedding garment." Well, we might think, maybe he didn't have one. No, the garments were supplied. Then (in the Orient) as now (in God's kingdom) they are freely available for all the guests.[3] Fortunately, we don't have to wonder what kind of garment we should put on. This same Book of Revelation tells us to prepare for the marriage supper by clothing ourselves with "the righteous deeds of the saints."[4] Word to the wise: We had better do it. Jesus' rebuked the believers of Sardis just as the king in His parable rebukes the hapless guest.

"But when the king came in to look at the guests, he saw there a man who had no wedding garment. And he said to him, 'Friend, how did you get in here without a wedding garment?' And he was speechless. Then the king said to the attendants, 'Bind him hand and foot and cast him into the outer darkness. In that place there will be weeping and gnashing of teeth.' For many are called, but few are chosen." Matthew 22:11-14

Revealed by Scripture

To the Church in Sardis

"And to the angel of the church in Sardis write: 'The words of him who has the seven spirits of God and the seven stars. "I know your works. You have the reputation of being alive, but you are dead. Revelation 3:1

Jesus greets the church of Sardis in His usual way by addressing the angelic overseer first.[5] Then according to form, He introduces Himself with a specific aspect of the fuller description which He had given to John as a prelude to his assignment. He wants the Sardis believers to know that He is the One who "has the seven spirits of God and the seven stars." He "has" them. The seven spirits and seven stars (angels) all belong to Him.[6] They are His. It is a polite reminder to the believers that they too belong to Him, yet there is no mention here of the churches. Previously, Jesus told John that the seven lampstands (churches) were in His "right Hand" along with the seven stars. Something seems amiss. The right Hand of God is always associated in scripture with His power to save, yet the church appears to have gone missing from it. So dire is the situation that Jesus skips over what always came next. His earlier pattern had been to give praise and encouragement to the church before raising points of criticism. Not this time.

Having begun in this veiled way, Jesus suddenly unveils an appalling sight. This group of believers sees itself as being alive in Christ, "but you are dead." What a stunner! There is no way that they could have seen that coming. According to Jesus they had been working hard to create a very different impression, but He knew their "works." He knew them as dead works. These are the things we do which aren't sins in the usual sense, certainly not sins like the ones He faulted Thyratira for doing: sexual immorality and eating food dedicated to idols.

The tragedy of dead works is that they are "good" things that we do in vain (futile, self-motivated, faith-less) attempts to please God and others. God is not pleased with us trying to please Him because He's already gone to great lengths to give us His favor—by punishing His Son. Faith assures us that He loves us first.[7] If we have trouble believing that truth, we are meant to work on our faith by building it up, rather than work on God by buttering Him up with things we think will please Him.

People pleasing is just as bad. The harder we work at trying to keep everybody happy, the less happy we become. The harder we try to get respect, the less respected we are. We may be doing all the right things, but the motive is wrong. We are serving self, not our Savior. Even if we don't know it, He does. The problem comes by believing our own press—if we succeed in making a good impression on others. They will praise us to the skies. We'll "have a reputation of being alive." But in Jesus eyes the life of faith has died.

Wake up, and strengthen what remains and is about to die, for I have not found your works complete in the sight of my God. Revelation 3:2

This alarming message is meant to "wake up" a sleeping Bride. Deception is like being asleep. Often, we don't know we're asleep, until someone tries to wake us. If we're deep asleep, they may have to shout and shake us. When that happens, we don't always wake up in a friendly mood! How did the Sardis believers awaken? Did they awaken? We're only getting the out-going letter, not the return mail. So, we simply don't know. Still, it's hard to overhear this conversation and not wake up ourselves. They probably did too. After all, it's Jesus who's doing the shouting. And the tenor of His message doesn't change. His voice remains loud and clear through to the end of the letter.

Now that they've awakened, He wants them to "strengthen what remains." Why, Lord? "It's about to die." Their works—their daily striving to do good on their terms—are dead works. They've been dead asleep coddled by sweet dreams of deception, thinking they were alive. Worse, even more things in their life are about to die on the vine. How to strengthen those things? Reconnect to the Vine that gives life! Jesus told us that apart from Him—the true Vine—we can do nothing.[8] Why don't we believe it?

Like the believers of Sardis, we, too, unplug from His life and leadership and busy ourselves chasing the phantom promise of finding peace apart from trusting obedience. There is only one way: His way. There is no peace in the heart if we depart. So, the word comes to return, reconnect and be renewed. Jesus has not found our "works complete." There is yet one thing missing. It is the best part, but we let it be taken from us.[9] The works could be fully good, if only He were at the center of them. The "incomplete" piece, the missing piece, is His peace.

Remember, then, what you received and heard. Keep it, and repent. If you will not wake up, I will come like a thief, and you will not know at what hour I will come against you. Revelation 3:3

Each of these letters is unique, tailored to fit a different set of believers every time. However, one part is beginning to sound like a broken record: "repent." The problem isn't with Jesus not having any other ideas to offer. This is the one and only solution. We're the ones with long-playing records of waywardness. It's time to break our record and play a new song, a song of faithful dedication to our God. That's what Jesus wants to hear from this Body of believers: The Song of the Bride.[10]

So, He tells them to "remember"—re-join your members to your true Head. Remember "what you received and heard" and (tell you what), just "keep it." The truth is that we have already been told what we need to do: trust Him, cling to Him, and "repent" every time we drift away. Yet, we keep seeking a "fresh word from God" as the answer to current problems thinking that more knowledge will save us. That's feeding on the wrong tree! Jesus is the tree of life planted in the garden of our heart. The same old word works great every time: repent.

If they don't repent, there will be repercussions. It is not Jesus' preferred way to "come like a thief"—that's the way of the Enemy. But for those who "will not wake" there is no other remedy than to give the bed a great shaking. The deep sleeper never knows the hours that are passing. Likewise, Jesus will come upon those sunk into deception's dark slumber at an hour they "will not know." There is no way to telegraph the punch to someone with their eyes closed. Whatever comes "against" them (against the wrong direction they are going) will hit them hard. Even so, the jolt is still intended to awaken, not to slay—to destroy their sleep, but not their hope.

Yet you have still a few names in Sardis, people who have not soiled their garments, and they will walk with me in white, for they are worthy. Revelation 3:4

Even when we are unfaithful, God is still faithful. One of the ways we see His faithfulness is through the remnant He preserves. Elijah thought he alone in Israel was standing up for the Lord against Ahab and Jezebel, but the Lord had a remnant of 7000 who had not "bowed the knee to Baal."[11] Time and again in Israel's long history of hope and failure, the Lord preserved a faithful few who carried faith's seed forward or at least kept it from losing further ground.

He has in Sardis "a few names" who have remained faithful. By saying "names" rather than "people" as we would expect, the Lord is ascribing honor. Certainly, He can name names when it comes to ascribing dishonor, as He did when He called out Thyatira's Jezebel. Far more frequently in scripture, He uses the giving of a name to convey that a person is no longer living out their birth name but living up to the new name that only He knows—the one He told the Pergamum believers about.

These faithful believers are making a name for themselves in heaven's sight. They are doing two "works" right. First, they have not "soiled their garments" through sin or the dead "works" that others had done. Second, they walked with Him in the unsullied "white" garment of salvation which the Bridegroom gives to every wedding guest. Their covering is the Lord's righteousness, not one of their own making. Their great work, so unlike the dead works first mentioned, is trusting everything in life to Jesus' great work of redemption. Their pleasure in Him is shown by how they "walk" with Him. This is what pleases Jesus. By ascribing such worth to Him, He calls them "worthy." The letter began with a stunning rebuke. Now we hear an equally stunning word of praise.

The one who conquers will be clothed thus in white garments, and I will never blot his name out of the book of life. I will confess his name before my Father and before his angels. Revelation 3:5

Just as the remnant at Sardis triumphed in life through faith, Jesus now promises "white garments" like theirs to all who conquer.[12] John would know for he wrote it in his first letter, that our victory—the victory that "overcomes the world"— always comes through our faith.[13] Jesus is the ultimate overcomer: He has overcome the world. It is our believing in Him that allows the miracle of grace to happen. He overcomes our little worlds of toil and trouble through us. Such faith is born of believing to the point of truly trusting and fully obeying Him. Such conquering gains life, His life. So, the promise He gives is the inevitable outcome of such a life: "I will never blot out his name from the book of life." The "book of life" is where the records are kept. May the old broken record of our past be forever blotted out and our new name be forever recorded!

He who has an ear, let him hear what the Spirit says to the churches.' Revelation 3:6

Catch the present tense. With God, all His Word is present tense. It is a word to be lived now, in today's day of salvation. Any word from back then can suddenly leap off the pages right now with a compelling call to faith and action. You may have to read between the lines to see Him winking at you or listen closely to hear His beckoning call. These, however, come pointed directly to our ears. Jesus knows He is speaking to us. He knows that His words to Sardis are being forever recorded in His Word. Even so, He doesn't command us to listen. It's an invitation: "He who has ears, let him hear." What He would like us to listen for is not what the Spirit said to Sardis and the other churches, but what the Spirit "says." Catch the wink and listen. What is He saying to you?

CHAPTER 8

THE SIXTH CHURCH: PHILADELPHIA

Revelation 3:7-13

The battle for faith is ultimately a battle for love. God is love. Because of His love the Father sent Jesus into the world so that everyone can be saved who yields to Him in trusting obedience. Not forced obedience, but a willing submission to the truth. Love would have it no other way. The great tragedy is that so much hatred surrounds this effort to bring divine Love to the earth. And that so many try to force their religious beliefs on others. Religious zeal can be fired up red hot in the entire absence of love. This often makes religion an enemy of the true spiritual life. The believers in Philadelphia know it only too well.

Because you have kept my word about patient endurance, I will keep you from the hour of trial that is coming on the whole world, to try those who dwell on the earth. Revelation 3:10

Chief Characteristics

Travelers, commerce and correspondence from Greece or Italy would arrive at Asia Minor's major seaport, Ephesus, then journey up the coast towards Pergamum, before turning east on the interior highway to Laodicea. The letter to the church at Philadelphia would have been the sixth letter delivered.

Irony hardly begins to describe the level of hatred that existed in this city of "brotherly love." Things started well. The city was founded in the second century BC by one brother out of love for another. King Eumenes of Pergamum established the city out of the largess of his own, then passed it on to his brother Attalus II who succeeded him. Attalus' loyalty to Eumenes was such that his nickname became *Philadelphos*— "one who loves his brother."[1] A good name and a good beginning are hard to keep unsullied.

By the late first century, a group of religious extremists began hating others in the city for not believing the same things they did. If this sounds familiar, it should. It is the story of the two seeds. The good seed here are the faithful believers in the true Messiah. Jesus called the seeds sown by the Enemy in Philadelphia "the synagogue of Satan." Deceived Jewish believers attacked those they should have been learning from. Deceived zealots will also be springing up around us in the days to come. They won't have the same religious beliefs as these, but they will have the same devil driving them from behind.

Pre-Figured in Scripture

Paul: The Conversion of a Zealot

The account of Paul's conversion is so important that we are told it three times in the Book of Acts. It made a huge impression on the first believers and it still makes one on us. He went from being Saul, the foremost persecutor of Christians, to becoming Paul, the greatest apostle for Christ. Prior to Paul's conversion, no one would have thought such a whole-life transformation possible. Good Jews and God-fearing Gentiles had become believers in Jesus, but they had already been taking a friendly stance towards the new thing God was doing. Saul wanted to destroy it!

Some images in our minds are indelibly etched. We can practically see Saul's anger as he headed towards Damascus, "still breathing threats and murder."[2] Then came the blinging light that knocked him to the ground. Then came the words that pierced him to the heart: "Saul, Saul, why are you persecuting me?"[3] Blinded physically by the revealing light as he had been blinded spiritually by deception, Paul awaited his fate for three days. His world had been completely turned upside down. Then came the miracle of grace. Jesus restored him to sight, gifted him and sent him out with a new assignment. The rest reads like a legend—he blazed such a path that it was said of him that he "turned the world upside down."[4]

What was the incubator for this scoundrel turn saint? Religion! The back story that we need to see are all the years of devotion that went into Saul's formation. Born Jewish, of the tribe of Benjamin, he sought to be preeminent among the Pharisees, the "reforming" group within Judaism. He didn't take his faith lightly. He fully believed in the God of the Bible. He was determined to live as devoted as he could, saying later that he was "blameless" at keeping the Law's righteous demands.[5] Yet, all this zeal for God was "not according to knowledge" for it lacked understanding of God's way of making us righteous.[6] He became on the inside a mini "synagogue of Satan" without ever once realizing it. That's why he is the perfect precursor to the persecutors we will see in this letter.

For you have heard of my former life in Judaism, how I persecuted the church of God violently and tried to destroy it. Galatians 1:13

Revealed by Scripture

To the Church in Philadelphia

"And to the angel of the church in Philadelphia write: 'The words of the holy one, the true one, who has the key of David, who opens and no one will shut, who shuts and no one opens. Revelation 3:7

As He has done previously, Jesus begins by honoring "the angel of the church" in Philadelphia.[7] If we aren't careful to think biblically, rather than culturally, our minds might picture an angel standing in or hovering over a church building. After so many centuries of seeing Christians meet within sacred walls on Sundays, buildings are the primary association we have for the Church. Not only that but the great cathedrals are far better known as edifices than for any facts or insights about the people who worshipped within them. Yet, people are the Church, believing people gathered in the Name of the Lord, so that Jesus can dwell in their midst as He promised.[8] Apart from the believers there is not a church, only an empty shell. Perhaps the name of this church, Philadelphia, should tip us off for it means brotherly love. That's the true church building—building one another up in love.[9]

Jesus begins straight away by laying a foundational revelation for this Body of believers. He introduces Himself with words full of hope and promise. He is the "holy one" and the "true one." Holiness speaks of the absolute purity of God's Being. He is completely unlike us in the He is utterly, unapproachably holy, but we are also like Him in that He is love. Unlike ours, however, His love is holy and pure. It is only by His grace that our love is being raised and refined to become ever more like His. His love is not only pure, it is true. He is the faithful Lover of souls we can depend upon to be true to His Word and true to us. This is a promise that the One speaking loves His Bride with a pure, perfect and everlasting love.

He brings with Him not only a loving Heart, but the power and authority needed by His Bride for she certainly has a way of getting into trouble. Not all her problems are her own doing as we shall see, but she needs her Lord's help often. It is just as easy (it seems) to be caught in the bondage of sin as it is to be barricaded by the Enemy with no apparent way to go forward. Never fear—Jesus has the keys. Earlier He told John that He had "the keys of Death and Hades." Those keys will set any fallen believer free from sin and guilt. Now, He reveals that he also holds "the key of David." This asserts His authority as Messiah over the Davidic kingdom—nothing an enemy can do will now stops its advance or bring it down to lasting defeat. There will be more on this in the next section.

"'I know your works. Behold, I have set before you an open door, which no one is able to shut. I know that you have but little power, and yet you have kept my word and have not denied my name. Revelation 3:8

Jesus condenses the sentence or two of affirmation He had given to the first four churches into this one little phrase: "I know your works." In His previous message to the believers in

Sardis, Jesus also told them that He knew their works—but those works were dead in His sight. That letter did not go well for them. It's different here. In saying He knew their works without faulting them, He is affirming them. If that feels slender, it is, but that's just the way it is walking with this divine Man. He knows only too well how quickly praise goes to our heads. So, it is that many times (in truth, nearly all the time) He will keep silent about how you're doing. His silence usually means you're doing well.

Next, He takes up the theme of David's key. Jesus knows that they "have but little power." That's why it is so helpful for us that He does. With the key of David, Jesus "opens [doors] and no one will shut." He also "shuts and no one opens" (vs. 7). His power over access and entry, over path and plan, is absolute. If He wants us with Him forever (and He does) then there is no other power or person who can block the way. That door—the very gate to heaven—is open. In the same way, He has forever closed off hell from those who cling to Him in trusting obedience. No need to fear that a stumbling will cause us to fall there, if we keep calling on Him as we go along.[10] That door is shut—even the devil himself can't drag a believer through it.

This remarkable ability with doors comes to our rescue in countless other ways. The advance of the kingdom can happen through such mundane things as jobs, as well as opportunities for ministry. It is not always clear which way to go. At other times when we have a sense of direction, the doors can seem shut against us. One powerful prayer is for Jesus to close doors that we don't need to walk through and to hold the one open that we do. Combined with asking Him to guide us to it, this prayer works wonders. We truly have but "little power" to open and close doors, less to discern the way—without His gracious interventions. Fortunately, our Davidic "doorkeeper" gladly intervenes if He can confess to the Father that we have "kept my word and have not denied my name."

Behold, I will make those of the synagogue of Satan who say that they are Jews and are not, but lie—behold, I will make them

come and bow down before your feet, and they will learn that I have loved you. Revelation 3:9

Now comes the showdown. This is the battle that necessitated a letter packed with so much encouragement. Spiritual warfare is arrayed against the believers. "The synagogue of Satan" has mounted an attack. That's strong language but Jesus isn't into name calling, only identity revealing. This is a Jewish synagogue which is arrayed against them, though it's not clear in what way. Jesus did forewarn that a time was coming when "they will put you out of the synagogues. Indeed, the hour is coming when whoever kills you will think he is offering service to God."[11] That time seems to have arrived in Philadelphia.

These spiritually mis-guided zealots "say that they are Jews and are not." They are judging themselves by their human ancestry, but Jesus is judging by what's in the heart. He would agree with Paul that "no one is a Jew who is merely one outwardly."[12] The true circumcision which marks a true Jew is "of the heart" and that is found in those who "worship by the Spirit of God and glory in the Lord Jesus Christ."[13] That's what these faithful believers are doing in Philadelphia and it is for this cause that they are being persecuted by the unconverted Jewish community. Jesus plans to convert them, or at least get them to confess the same truth that Saul of Tarsus heard when he was hounding Christians to death: "Saul, Saul, why are you persecuting Me?"[14] So, Jesus comforts His believers with this promise, that one day their enemies will "learn that I have loved you." He stands with (and in) His faithful followers.

Because you have kept my word about patient endurance, I will keep you from the hour of trial that is coming on the whole world, to try those who dwell on the earth. Revelation 3:10

The "patience endurance" of the Philadelphian believers will be rewarded. Patient endurance isn't sitting on one's hands waiting for the unwanted situation to change. It is going about one's business in the Lord advancing in the kingdom in every other area that can be changed. Neither is it the weary resignation that trudges on, dragging a heavy heart and little hope. No, the flame of hope is kept bright with a lively faith that God is going to come through one way or the other. What endures is the bright hope that God will have His way and the surrendered heart that says that's all that really matters. Otherwise, it's just white-knuckled hanging on.

To those who keep faith alive in the trial, Jesus promises that He will "keep you from the hour of trial." He doesn't say keep you faithful "in" the hour of trial but keep you "from" it. That poses a problem. Why would the reward for learning how to survive in a trial be not having to be in a trial? That would be like saying to a child, "Now that you've learned how to swim, I'll never take you to the pool again." It just doesn't make sense.

What makes more sense is that Jesus will bless this faith-ability to such a degree that future trials won't seem like trials at all. Everyone who has walked under Jesus' leadership for any length of time knows this by personal experience. Situations and people who used to try us down to our last nerve, no longer can get our goat. We've passed those tests so many times they no longer feel like trials at all. They did once, but the Spirit keeps us floating above them now.

If this interpretation is correct, then we have a template for the "trial that is coming on the whole world." In their day, that would have been the "worldwide" persecution which covered the whole Roman Empire—the only world they knew. Few areas where the Church had spread escaped the outward pressure of the trial. Perhaps, these Philadelphian believers passed through it without being torn apart on the inside by fear and doubt. Let's hope we can pass through our future trial with the same grace-based enduring faith. We know it's coming. Jesus said so: It's coming "to try those who dwell on the earth."[15] In the meantime, learn to make every trial count towards gaining "patient endurance." It will keep you safe in the Savior's grip of grace.

I am coming soon. Hold fast what you have, so that no one may seize your crown. Revelation 3:11

It is very hard to read the first four words of this verse without a wry smile stealing across one's face. Ok, sometimes it's a smirk. Have you ever wished you could go back and revise an estimate? When Jesus said through Isaiah that His thoughts are not our thoughts, He wasn't kidding![16] I thought (as the Early Church did) that "soon" meant in a year or two, tops. Evidently, that was not the thought in Jesus' mind. On the other hand, if the universe you created required 13.8 billion years (as scientists believe), and you had to wait that long to finally get to do what you popped the cork on the Big Bang to do—create man—then maybe for you, two thousand years goes by a bit too soon.

Or, it could be that we've taken a phrase like this out of context. Jesus says the same thing in Revelation 22:12 and there He is clearly talking about His Return. Here, He is telling the Philadelphian believers, "Hold on, I'm coming." That could only mean that He would be showing up in their lifetime. Otherwise, why make the promise to them? But we have seen several times already how Jesus uses these letters to them to speak to us.

The rest of this word also applies to us as well as them: "Hold fast what you have." He's not referring to material goods. That would be entirely out of Character. What they are to keep secure (as He keeps them secure) are things like "faith, hope and love."[17] If they can keep these well in hand as they pass through their trials, then their crown can't be seized from them. Jesus doesn't name the crown He has in mind, though previously He promised the "crown of life" to the believers in Smyrna, if they proved likewise faithful in their trial. We know only two things about it: Whatever it is, it's worth having if Jesus wants to give it and we'll love it when we see it in heaven. Oh, and a third thing would be that someone out there wants to "seize" it from us.

The one who conquers, I will make him a pillar in the temple of my God. Never shall he go out of it, and I will write on him the name of my God, and the name of the city of my God, the new Jerusalem, which comes down from my God out of heaven, and my own new name. Revelation 3:12

Jesus strikes a consistent chord in these messages. It is the blaring sound of a war trumpet. He sees His believers as embattled by dark powers spearheaded by Satan, even if they (we) don't. As often as we hear the word repent, we hear conquer. Repent speaks of bowing before the Lord, so He can raise us up. Repentance, therefore, calls to mind one's personal devotional and moral life—turn back to God and things will go better for you. That's certainly true and is perhaps the primary way most believers nowadays see it. However, Jesus sees life as a battle which we are meant to actively engage. We are to stand and fight against the Enemy, not just bow before God. Prayer is talking to God. Spiritual warfare is addressing the Enemy. We need both.

Along these lines, Jesus promises "to the one who conquers" that he shall be made "a pillar in the temple of my God." The one who bows before God in repentance and stands against the Enemy's onslaught is already a pillar to the Church—the Body of believers he/she lives among. Jesus says that this reality on earth is matched by a corresponding reality in heaven. Just as the ones who conquer uphold the Church, so they are seen in heaven as those who uphold true worship which the temple represents. It is not enough to worship the Lord on Sundays, if we fail to stand firm during the trials of life the rest of the week. That's the true test of devotion.

Further promises are given. It should be abundantly clear by now that although the Lord loves everyone equally and His love is unconditional, His promises have specific conditions attached. Those who reach into this book to pull promises out like candy from a box would be wise not to pull those promises out of context. The context for these promises is "the one who conquers." Only conquerors—also called overcomers—will receive the two names mentioned next: "the name of my God" and "the name of the city of my God."

While it is true that every biological son or daughter is a child of their father, there is a sense by which the child who most perfectly reflects all that is in the father, is a "true child" of the man. We see this even with Jesus when the writer of

Hebrews quotes Psalm 2:7 which has the Father saying to the Messiah: "You are my son; today I have begotten you." He tells us that this is in the context of Jesus' faithfulness to God at the cross. As God Jesus is always God's Son. However, as the carpenter from Nazareth, Jesus was raised after the cross to a higher rank than "angels as the name he has inherited is more excellent than theirs."[18] Incredibly, as fully Man, Jesus had been made "for a little while lower than the angels."[19] Just as Jesus received a new name due to His faithfulness, so will the overcomers.

A second name to be inscribed (a heavenly tattoo?) upon overcomers will be the name of God's holy city Jerusalem. This is the first time in the book that this astounding future event is revealed. The Jerusalem "that is above" one day "comes down from my God out of heaven."[20] There will be more on this later in the book. For now, let's recall that the location of a person's birth is recorded by the Lord: "And of Zion it shall be said, 'This one and that one were born in her'; for the Most High himself will establish her." By the new birth and by their faithfulness in living the new life that it makes possible, overcovers will be "named" as being born of Jerusalem no matter where their biological birth took place. In addition, Jesus says that He will also give them His "own new name"—the one we just reviewed with the help of the author of Hebrews.

He who has an ear, let him hear what the Spirit says to the churches.' Revelation 3:13

This is an urgent message to believers everywhere— "the churches." Once again, we are reading these letters incorrectly, if we think that they were only directed to seven churches in Asia Minor and have no bearing on us or our times. It is entirely possible that we will need the wisdom, rebukes, encouragement and insights they contain more than any generation before us, including the originally addressees. Ears, listening ears, are what's called for, not just biological ones. Without a sincere desire to hear and a willingness to truly listen, who will "hear what the Spirit says"? It certainly won't be the complacent whose tragic condition will be addressed in the next and final letter.

THE SEVENTH CHURCH: LAODICEA

Revelation 3:14-22

The church of Laodicea is easily the most famous of the Seven Churches in the Book of Revelation. That's not because Jesus saved the best for last. They were indeed last—last in line on the mail route and lagging way behind at running faith's race. In fact, they weren't running, or even walking with Jesus or towards Him. They weren't running away either, or even running to the devil. He said He could have worked with any of that. What were they doing? They were "living the dream"—using His blessings to feather their own nest. They thought they had it made, but they couldn't have been more wrong. Many have said that the Church in America fits this picture all too well.

"I know your works: you are neither cold nor hot. Would that you were either cold or hot! So, because you are lukewarm, and neither hot nor cold, I will spit you out of my mouth." Revelation 3:15-16

Chief Characteristics

Travelers, commerce and correspondence from Greece or Italy would arrive at Asia Minor's major seaport, Ephesus, then journey up the coast towards Pergamum, before turning east on the interior highway to Laodicea. The letter to the church at Laodicea would have been the seventh letter delivered.

Laodicea sits at the end of the route that would have been traversed by anyone taking mail from Patmos to the other six cities addressed by these letters. Founded in the 3rd century BC, Laodicea became an important commercial center due to its position on the trade road connecting the coastal ports with the resources of Asia Minor's interior. By the 12 century AD it became deserted due to warfare between the Byzantines and Seljuq Turks. Earthquakes in the 18th and 19th centuries completed its destruction.[1]

Jesus knew this city well. When He spoke of hot and cold, He was pointing to the unique geography surrounding Laodicea. From city center one can see six miles to the north the hillside where ancient Hierapolis drew crowds to its famous hot springs and baths. Not far off, Mount Gokbel stands to high elevation (7,572 feet) and sends its cold waters into the Menderes River, then down the valley leading towards Laodicea. Hot and cold close at hand, yet the believers here were lukewarm. Jesus threatened to "spew them" out of his mouth if things didn't change. Standing amid the present-day ruins, it is impossible to find a single building that has more than a fraction of its stone walls intact. For scores of acres all around, the countryside is covered with broken building stones — exactly as if some giant had chewed on them a while and spit them out. It is a lamentable and sobering sight.

Pre-Figured in Scripture

Esau: Despising His Inheritance

Is there someone in scripture who was lukewarm? Was there someone who had been offered an incredible inheritance, yet grew lackadaisical about it? Indeed, there was! And this was not just any inheritance but "the" inheritance. The seed line for the Messiah and the promise to Abraham were given to Esau. He didn't even have to work to get it — it was given to him at birth. He only had to work to keep it. That's sort of like us. We are granted salvation as a free gift at our new birth, but in some way have to "work out" our salvation through a process known as sanctification.[2] That's what Paul said he did and what we should do as well.[3] Apparently, the Laodicean Christians didn't agree. Neither did this character. But they should have paid attention to his example. It's a life lesson in what not to do.

As it happened, Esau had a brother who was desperate to the get that inheritance. To be sure, he was striving in the flesh. He was a usurper and a deceiver. But he knew a good thing when he saw it. Jacob went after the inheritance ninety to nothing. Now, you would think that should disqualify him — he really was an incorrigible rascal. Jesus, however, saw that Jacob was hot—that won the divine approval. When Esau proved he "despised" his inheritance by trading it for a bowl of porridge, he lost his position in salvation history. The lentils may have been hot, but he was lukewarm. That's not what Jesus is looking for!

Jacob said, "Sell me your birthright now." Esau said, "I am about to die; of what use is a birthright to me?" Jacob said, "Swear to me now." So he swore to him and sold his birthright to Jacob. Then Jacob gave Esau bread and lentil stew, and he ate and drank and rose and went his way. Thus Esau despised his birthright. Genesis 25:31-34

Revealed by Scripture

To the Church in Laodicea

"And to the angel of the church in Laodicea write: 'The words of the Amen, the faithful and true witness, the beginning of God's creation. Revelation 3:14

The letter begins in the usual way, but don't let that fool you. Jesus acknowledges "the angel of the church of Laodicea" exactly as He has done six times before.[4] But something's coming. Something they won't want to hear—not unless they have the kind of wisdom Solomon recommends: "It is better for a man to hear the rebuke of the wise than to hear the song of fools."[5] Something tells us that if they had that kind of wisdom, they wouldn't have wound up in the predicament about to unfold. This is reading ahead so we can be prepared.

Coming back to the text, Jesus says He is "the Amen, the faithful and true witness." We know that He is faithful and true from the rest of scripture which describes His nature and His steadfast ways. However, these two titles are unique to this book. Jesus calls Himself the Amen and the Witness. Amen is a Hebrew word that signifies something, someone or some statement is faithful, reliable or established.[6] As such it is used over one hundred times in the Bible. Jesus takes the word and applies it to Himself. His is the big Amen behind every little amen.

Jesus says that He is also "the" faithful witness. He is the ultimate Witness behind all true witnesses. Many have witnessed about what they've seen in Him, including the Father. What is He a witness to? He who is Truth told Pilate that He came "to bear witness to the truth."[7] He is the One who brings the light of heaven's truth into every dark nook and cranny where falsehood tries to hide.

Having said He is the Witness, Jesus tacks on a closing thought that seems a bit out of step. He is "the beginning of God's creation." How did we get there? Certainly, creation began with Jesus and He was there in the beginning.[8] However, considering the previous two titles this may be an allusion to how creation began—on a foundation of truth that was well-established, faithful and reliable. He is coming back to correct what went wrong, what grew false. That would include the believers in Laodicea.

15 "'I know your works: you are neither cold nor hot. Would that you were either cold or hot! 16 So, because you are lukewarm, and neither hot nor cold, I will spit you out of my mouth. Revelation 3:15-16

Without any fanfare, Jesus lowers the boom. There is not a single word of encouragement or recognition preceding what comes next. It's a blistering rebuke: "I know your works: you are neither cold nor hot." This puts such a bad taste in His mouth that He warns, "I will spit you out of my mouth." That is not something any believer wants to hear. We secretly hope to hear Him say, "Well done good and faithful servant."[9] Not, "What have you done? You faithless servant!" Nevertheless, these are the words scorching the Laodicean ears. How can they bear it? The Lord's indignation is hot against them because they are "lukewarm." If His words don't light a fire under them nothing will.

Hot and cold (or cold and hot) appear together three times in this one verse. The repetition carries meaning. Holy, holy, holy is heaven's refrain. Anything scripture repeats three times has special significance. In the back of one's mind the Trinity faintly echoes through this pattern. Could it be that these apathetic believers are neither hot nor cold towards the Father, the Son, or the Holy Spirit? Is not One of the Godhead worthy of either their attention or their ire?

We say of outstanding personalities we know that "you'll either love them or hate them" to friends who haven't met them yet. CS Lewis wrote that if you can stand in front of a beautiful sunset or the Mona Lisa and feel nothing, there's something wrong. That's what Jesus is getting at. How can these believers have been introduced to Jesus who died for them and say, "Oh well, been there, done that"? How can the God in heaven be made known as their loving Father and final Judge and they let the connection go dead? How can the Holy Spirit be living within them, ready to guide them into truth and life and they could care less?

We see what's at stake, but they don't. Are they trying to navigate a middle path? Some call it being "inoculated" by the gospel—just enough Christianity to get you feeling safe and saved, but not enough to be a bother. We saw in the previous letter the peril of what too much religion can do when zeal goes off track. But zeal has a good side, too. It's been said that a religious fanatic is someone who loves Jesus more than you do. Trying to avoid extremes can become extremely compromising.

Jesus would rather see extremes, than a muddled, complacent middle. He would see hot: Someone in hot pursuit of Him, passionate even if a bit mis-guided. Or He would see cold: Someone who has shut Him out and barred the door and is making no pretense about it. What He hates is the hypocrisy that pretends to be good but disregards Him. Where's the goodness in that? Worse, He seems to be saying that it's harder for Him to work with lukewarm pretenders, than notorious sinners or zealous fanatics. At least if you're on the go He can guide you or turn you around, but if you've stopped dead in the water…

For you say, I am rich, I have prospered, and I need nothing, not realizing that you are wretched, pitiable, poor, blind, and naked. Revelation 3:17

Complacency is their problem. In their eyes they've arrived. No need to press on or press in for a higher prize.[10] They're saying to themselves, "I am rich, I have prospered, and I need nothing." What? Don't they "need" to be living their lives for Jesus, rather than themselves? Don't they need to be forging a lasting relationship with Him? Perhaps they're taking their present blessings as a sign that He's pleased with them. They couldn't be more wrong! In His eyes they're "wretched, pitiable, poor, blind, and naked." In the normal course of things, anyone in such dreadful conditions would be exactly the sort of person Jesus wants to save. But they're "saved" already!

Now we see the problem they don't see. If only they knew how miserable their condition is in God's sight, they would be crying out for help. Usually, the average person being readied for salvation, feels how desperate their condition is and calls on God. These "saved" believers need Jesus just as desperately as when they first began, but they don't feel the need, nor do they see it. That's why Jesus is "shouting" at them. He has to shock them into "realizing" their reality.

I counsel you to buy from me gold refined by fire, so that you may be rich, and white garments so that you may clothe yourself and the shame of your nakedness may not be seen, and salve to anoint your eyes, so that you may see. Revelation 3:18

Now that He has their attention, He can offer remedies with each one shaped to match their need. Again, it should be noted that this is the Bride Jesus loves despite her blemishes. For this reason, He's not making demands. Instead, He offers "counsel." Because they're poor in the real treasures, He recommends buying "gold refined by the fire." During His Galilee days, Jesus warned us not to "store up treasures on earth" but only those in heaven.[11]

Jesus didn't explain what the heavenly treasures are then or now, but we can speculate. These would be the things we can take with us or those that will be given to us there. Anyone we work with Him to save—whether family member, friend or stranger—will be a genuine treasure we can "take" with us. So, will any and all virtues He works into our character, including wisdom, knowledge and skill. Heaven will supply us with treasures of reward—the crowns He keeps mentioning are only a part of it—for all the good we do under His leadership. Even so, the greatest treasure will be the level of intimacy we reach with Him here—that will somehow set the tone or the starting point of our intimacy with Him there. He is the highest treasure and heaven's greatest reward.

Jesus prefers to see His beloved Bride properly clothed. We saw this same concern expressed in His letter to Sardis and investigated it there. Here, we see that the underlying problem for them (as for us) is their "nakedness." Ever since the debacle of Eden nakedness in public is a sign of original disgrace, not innocence. We cannot go back to that. Indeed, whatever may have been the first plan is a thing forever covered up before our ever-curious eyes. When we peer into heaven by the light of scripture, we see everyone fully clothed there. Why was it "good' for Adam and Eve to be without clothes? How could it have continued? Could it have continued into heaven? We'll never know. We know for certain, however, that it's not good for us to be naked.

Our spiritual garments are of two kinds, because our nakedness is of two kinds. There is the shame of sin. There is also the shame of our brokenness, which includes our wide-ranging weakness and ignorance, our wounds and inabilities. The garment of salvation covers our sin. We are "covered" by the Blood of Jesus. God our Father sees the Blood covering us and we're good to go. This is widely taught. The other covering we need is not as well understood. He gives us the robe of His Righteousness to cover our shameful inability to show forth any righteousness of our own. Where the Blood covers our sinfulness, His Righteousness covers our weakness.

To the robes, Jesus adds salve to "anoint" our eyes. Without the holy scriptures and the Holy Spirit, we are blind as bats. The salve that saves is the anointing of the Spirit combined with the reading of His Word. It takes both to restore spiritual sight. Our condition is such that this needs to be done daily. We don't just need to see Jesus well enough to get to heaven. That seems to have been part of the Laodicean problem. We need to see even more what it is that Jesus our Lord wants us to do every day, so that He can lead us to heaven step by faithful step.

Those whom I love, I reprove and discipline, so be zealous and repent. Revelation 3:19

Here comes the desired fire. Since the flame has gone out, the solution is to "be zealous and repent." It's fine to pray while walking, sitting or lying in bed, but this calls for hitting the knees, or possibly lying prone. Realize how badly you need to repent and pray like you mean it. Put your heart into it. This is called being awakened by the holy fear of God and it is a good thing. Fear of the fire of hell will put the fire of love into you for anyone who will save you from it. They had forgotten how badly they needed saving. They don't need saving from Jesus or from the Father—He loves those whom He "reproves and disciplines." They need saving by Him. They had been letting go of His Hand and were drifting from His saving embrace. Thinking you're saved eternally, when you're doing nothing on your end. That's being lukewarm. That's spiritual danger.

Behold, I stand at the door and knock. If anyone hears my voice and opens the door, I will come in to him and eat with him, and he with me. Revelation 3:20

This verse is often used by evangelists and that's fine. It's true and it works splendidly. The lost have the door of their heart shut to the Lord and don't know how to open it. As they hear His "voice" speaking to them through the gospel, they unlock that door. As they open to Him, Jesus comes in. Then table fellowship abounds as the new convert shares with Him the living bread of divine truth and the joy-inducing wine of the covenant—the forgiveness of sins. That's great. In fact, it's out of this world. It's also taken out of context.

Jesus isn't speaking to the lost here. He is addressing believers who gather to worship Him in Laodicea in full knowledge of who He is. Well, they do at least know Him as Savior. If they knew Him well enough, they would be expending every ounce of strength and moment of time to get to know Him better. To know Him is to love Him. To love Him is to want to know Him better. This is the never-ending circle of divine fire that Jesus wants to see burning in the hearts of His followers. He's not seeing it here.

As elsewhere in the letters, Jesus is casting His words through that past time to ours. To "anyone" who hears His voice He issues this call to come up higher. That can include the lost, of course, but we need to be very clear about the context— lest we fall into the sad plight of these lax Laodiceans. Jesus says He is standing outside His own church. He is "at the door" and knocking, hoping they will hear and let Him in. He can't or won't "come in" unless we do as He desires: throw the door of our heart wide. Yield our lives entirely to His will. Turn over the operations of our church to Him.

The one who conquers, I will grant him to sit with me on my throne, as I also conquered and sat down with my Father on his throne. Revelation 3:21

It takes fire to live at this level. It takes faith, love and hope that are fixed entirely on Jesus. As we have heard Him say to the other churches, it also takes listening, repenting, holding fast and obeying. There is much to conquer! The world, the flesh and the devils all require special handling. This is not a game the lukewarm can drift through playing half-heartedly. They don't even know it's going on. Others do. To those who hear this upward call and wake up, great things are promised. Jesus will grant His overcomers the right to "sit with me on my throne."

How did Jesus get His throne? We could say that He's had it from before time since He is God, but that would be the wrong answer. This is the throne of David, the throne of the Davidic kingdom. The One who sits on it holds David's key of authority as we saw in the letter to Philadelphia. Only a Man can be David's rightful heir and sit on David's throne. Jesus had to pass all the tests first—in His humanity—just as He is asking us to do. He also had to conquer under trials and against temptations all the way to the cross. Now, He wants us to do the same. Then we can join Him on His seat. Being seated speaks of rest—rest from trials. Sitting on a throne speaks of authority. Both will come to the overcomers.

He who has an ear, let him hear what the Spirit says to the churches.'" Revelation 3:22

With this final word of promise Jesus wraps up His letter with the now familiar phrase, "He who has an ear, let Him hear." We've heard it at the end of every letter, but we have also heard it before—long before. This is exactly what He said when describing John the Baptist to the crowds in Galilee and it fits wonderfully well into this context.

From prison John sent his disciples to ask Jesus, if He was the long-awaited Messiah. Jesus sent answer back by way of pointing to the supernatural works He was doing. Then, He turned to the crowds to give honor to John, saying that among those born of women there was none greater. Yet, John could only advance the kingdom. Not having the new birth, he couldn't enter it.[12] We can. Jesus said that "even the least in the kingdom" is (somehow) greater than John. We who have received the new birth are uniquely graced both to advance the kingdom and to enter it. According to Paul, that kingdom is "righteous, peace and joy in the Holy Spirit."[13]

This kingdom is our true inheritance on the earth, our Promised Land. Entering it is our daily calling—and our great delight. Advancing it into other lives is our great commission— and our highest duty. That won't happen without battles. This is heavily contested territory, otherwise every Christian would already be living in right ways, filled with peace and joy and fully empowered by the Holy Spirit. Jesus knows it. That's why

He told the crowds to prepare for war. Overcomers: You've got something to overcome!

From the days of John the Baptist until now the kingdom of heaven has suffered violence, and the violent take it by force... He who has ears to hear, let him hear. Matthew 11:12, 15

Signs of the Last Days

*"So also, when you see these things taking place,
you know that he [Jesus] is near,
at the very gates."*

Mark 13:29

UNPRECEDENTED SIGNS

Many of the signs Christians give as indications that Jesus is coming soon are not at all convincing to unbelievers.[1] They're not even convincing to many of us. Such things as weather events, or political crisis, or moral degeneration have always been happening somewhere on the earth (just as Jesus said they would). However, there are unprecedented Biblical signs—stupendous happenings prophesied in scripture—that are taking place now which have never taken place before. These signs silence even the skeptics.

But he answered them, "When it is evening, you say, 'It will be fair weather, for the sky is red.' In the morning, 'It will be foul weather today, for the sky is red and threatening.' Hypocrites! You know how to discern the appearance of the sky, but you can't discern the signs of the times! Matthew 16:2-3 WEB

Read and Heed the Signs!

Jesus' above rebuke is a strong one. The strength of it tells us that Jesus fully expected everyone to be able to read the "signs of the times" the first time He came to earth. Recall that there were many prophecies about Messiah's birth, life, work, and death recorded in the Hebrew scriptures. Nevertheless, many Jewish believers failed to recognize Him as Messiah, nor did any of them understand what had been foretold about His true calling.

Zoom forward to our day. There are vastly more prophecies and far more astonishing signs pointing to His Return, than to His first visit. His second coming is not merely an addendum to the cross. It will usher in the fulfilment of all that His death and resurrection began. He is returning to accomplish nothing short of the

---

[1] The articles in this "Bonus Section" are taken with permission from *Signs of the Last Days* also published by the author at Amazon.

"restoration of all things."[2] What will He say of this generation, if we don't read and heed the signs we've been given? Fortunately, certain of the signs are so fresh on the scene and so marvelous in nature that they carry a power to convince like nothing we've seen before.

Unique and Unarguable Signs

These signs are unique. None of the signs to be discussed were in place prior to the middle of the past century. This means that until very recently, no one looking for Biblical signs of the Lord's return could have said His Return was drawing near—not without ignoring scripture. None of these signs had even begun to occur until just over a hundred years ago. On the other hand, the signs of the "Birth Pains"—wars and natural disasters, for instance—have always been with us. These signs, on the other hand, never have been present on the earth. They are utterly unprecedented as signs of the Second Coming. Many of them are also unprecedented as never-before-seen historical events.

The recent appearance of these signs makes them extraordinary, but it also makes them unarguable. Sure, some skeptics will continue to scoff, but any honest observer would have to admit how astounding it is that so many prophecies from thousands of years ago exactly describe our times. Not only that but they include things about our times that would have been unthinkable, unimaginable realities to those who prophesied them.

Such a startling congruence of ancient prophecy and present events simply doesn't happen in ordinary history. This makes them incontrovertible. How can anyone argue against such a mountain of evidence? Even so, it may not convince unbelievers that it was our God who made the prophecies and who even now is fulfilling them. Without repentance and conversion, even glaringly obvious signs of divinity are written off by the hard-hearted as coincidence or irrelevant. Even so, they cannot deny the congruence of these signs, even if they choose to seek some other explanation for it. (Good luck with that!)

---

[2] Acts 3:21

For Christians, however, the convergence of these signs points inexorably to the knowledge that Jesus said His Church would have about the season of His Return. Most Christians believe deep down that these are the Last Days. These signs give us clear, solid Biblical evidence for that innate belief. Their "sudden" appearance in our generation is nothing short of miraculous. In every case, these signs represent prophecies in scripture that for two thousand years seemed, not only distant, but impossible. Now, there are not only visible, they are racing towards completion right before our awestruck eyes!

14 Unprecedented Signs

These "unprecedented and incontrovertible" signs fall under three main headings: Jewish Signs, Gospel Signs and Global Signs. Each of these groups contain numerous signs each.

1. Six Jewish Signs

It is a mark of God's faithfulness that He never forgets, but always fulfills, His promises and His purposes. Long before Jesus came to earth, God chose the Jewish people to be in a unique covenant relationship with Himself. This was certainly intended for their benefit, but also for ours: Ultimately the long-awaited Savior would come to them, then through them to us. Guess what? He is getting things ready to do it again! And His own beloved first covenant believers are already playing a major role.

2. Three Gospel Signs

Jesus gave us this sign, but Peter explained it. He wrote in 2 Peter 3:1-9 that the Father is in no hurry to bring things to a quick close because He doesn't want anyone to perish, but all to come to repentance. For that to happen the gospel has to be preached to all the world. That day is coming at us like a freight train... but there is more to this gospel sign than simply getting the word out.

3. Five Global Signs

When the Bible was being written the world to its authors was no larger than the Mediterranean basin and outlying provinces, mostly under Roman control. Before the entire world could be organized into anything like the unified whole pictured in the Book of Revelation, it first had to be explored, then subdued. When these signs were given, they were unthinkable possibilities; now they are everyday realities. Well, almost all…

An Orderly Flow of Events

These sign groupings are ordered in this way for a reason. Our scriptures tell us that the gospel is to the Jews first.[3] Curiously, the Jewish signs began appearing first, then the others followed. Not only that, but the Hebrew scripture prophecies concerning "The Day of the Lord" preceded the New Testament prophecies about the Last Days and speak much about God's future dealings with His first chosen people.

In this sense, the redemption coming to us all through the Lord's Return is for the Jews first. We Gentile believers would do well to honor their position in the heart and plan of the Lord. Through the Jews—through the Jewish Messiah, Jesus—this gospel came to us Gentiles. We in turn must pass it on to all the world. Those Jewish and gospel signs are now taking place within the context of a world that is rapidly being transformed globally, not entirely for the better. The Jews. The Gospel. The Globe. That's the unfolding progression of salvation, culminating soon in the Lord's Return.

---

[3] Romans 1:16

SIX JEWISH SIGNS

The Jewish people were chosen to be a sign, a pointer to the invisible reality of God and His otherwise inscrutable ways. Not just a sign, but also a reality—the visible expression of God's life and saving love in the world. Out of the very life of Israel has come everlasting life through their Messiah and ours. Jesus will forever be a Jewish man. He is fully God, but in His humanity, He was and remains Jewish.

They are Israelites, and to them belong the adoption, the glory, the covenants, the giving of the law, the worship, and the promises. To them belong the patriarchs, and from their race, according to the flesh, is the Christ who is God over all, blessed forever. Amen. Romans 9:4-5

The First Chosen

What kind of sign? For many benighted centuries, these first-chosen ones seemed, perhaps even to themselves, to be a warning sign: "At all costs, avoid God's disfavor!" Tevye, the beleaguered Jewish narrator in "The Fiddler on the Roof," joked half-seriously, "I know, I know. We are Your chosen people. But, once in a while, can't You choose someone else?" In the world's eyes, their light was buried under bushel baskets of misunderstanding, suspicion, and prejudice that we heaped upon them. All this is changing, changing so suddenly and dramatically that it is breath-taking to behold.

The Jewish people in one generation have gone from being obscure and despised on the fringes of every country, to being in command of one of the most dynamic nations in the world. Their scientists have garnered a preponderance of Nobel Prizes out of all proportion to their numbers. They are world-class leaders in technology and medicine as well as science. Even without oil, their economy consistently outperforms that of their less entrepreneurial neighbors. Yet, all this pales in comparison to role the Lord has chosen for them in the Last Days. The Returning King of the Earth will set up His throne and rule from Jerusalem in the heart of a restored Israel!

Naturally enough, with the kind of future He intends, the signs associated with modern Israel are, perhaps, the greatest evidence the Lord can give us of His preparations to return soon.

1) The Re-gathering of the Jews

The return of Jews to the land promised by God is a modern miracle. It also set the End Times clock in motion. The Lord promised the land to Abraham and his descendants *forever*. Every Christian knows this. Less well known is the sheer number of prophecies in the Old Testament which foretold a vast dispersal of the Jews following the loss of their homeland—that, and the subsequent work of the Lord which would restore them. Always, this restoration was couched in terms of "the latter days." Jesus proclaimed the same things.

They will fall by the edge of the sword and be led captive among all nations, and Jerusalem will be trampled underfoot by the Gentiles, until the times of the Gentiles are fulfilled. Luke 21:24

How were the Jews scattered? And why? The Roman Empire was the agent both of Israel's destruction and the Jewish dispersal. If you asked them, they would have said the nation was ungovernable. The First Jewish War began as a revolt. The Romans crushed it in typically brutal manner with the siege of Jerusalem and the destruction of the Temple (70 AD). The Second Revolt of Judea (132-135 AD) was the last straw. In putting down the rebellion led by Bar Kokhba, the Romans razed Jerusalem, desecrated the Temple mount, and raised a Roman city in its place. Jews of Judea were either killed, exiled, or sold into slavery. The centuries-long Diaspora had begun. This, too, was prophesied by a despondent Jesus:

"O Jerusalem, Jerusalem, the city that kills the prophets and stones those who are sent to it! How often would I have gathered your children together as a hen gathers her brood under her wings, and you were not willing! See, your house is left to you desolate." Matthew 23:37-38

A Slow Then Sudden Return

For well over a millennium and a half, Jews of the Diaspora (dispersal) prayed with yearning hearts to see a return to the land. No doubt the nearly universal persecution they experienced compounded their anguish at being outcasts and wanderers. Even so, they proved reluctant to leave the relative "security" of the ghetto for an uncertain future. Theodore Herzl, the founder of modern Zionism, correctly read the signs of antisemitism in the late 1800s. He called for European Jews to return to the Land, but the response was a trickle. Europe was civilized and safe. Far too few realized that the Zionists were the prophesied "fishers." The Nazi "hunters" came afterward.

But 'As the LORD lives who brought up the people of Israel out of the north country and out of all the countries where he had driven them.' For I will bring them back to their own land that I gave to their fathers. "Behold, I am sending for many fishers declares the LORD, and they shall catch them. And afterward I will send for many hunters, and they shall hunt them from every mountain and every hill, and out of the clefts of the rocks. Jeremiah 16:15-16

In the aftermath of the Holocaust and World War, the Zionist movement, led by David Ben-Gurion, grew ever more determined to regain Israel for the Jews. The Allied powers knew about the death camps yet refused to bomb the rail lines leading to them. If the Jews were to survive in such a hostile world, they vowed they would never go meekly to the slaughter again, as so many had in the gas chambers. Many lost all faith that they could count on God. They could only count on themselves. Sadly, just when Israel was reborn, their ancient faith lay in the grave (for all but the

Orthodox). To this day the majority of Israelis are adamantly secular, even if avowedly ethnic, in their outlook and allegiance.

We can be certain that the Lord has plans for a far fuller restoration than a mere return to the land. They have an ancient spiritual inheritance He intends to renew. For now, however, the Jews are in their Holy Land once again. After two thousand years of exile, that is—in itself—a massive sign of the Last Days!

2) The Restoration of the Hebrew Language

Of all the stupendous, amazing signs of His Return that the Lord gives through His first-chosen people, this one probably has the least impact on geo-political events. Yet it is no less dazzling. When in the full course of human events has a once-dead language ever been successfully brought back to life? To be sure, Latin and Greek are still taught, but outside the walls of the Vatican Latin is never spoken. The Greek of Greece is not the original tongue so eloquently written by Paul. Even the English of Shakespeare is practically a closed book to his linguistic descendants. Many old tongues have died off. None have been brought back to life. In recent times, the Irish Republic launched a heroic attempt to bring back ancient Gaelic. It failed.

Yet, Israel speaks Biblical Hebrew once again. Let that sink in. The entire nation not only speaks Hebrew which, like Latin and Greek, had been a language kept alive on life-support solely for religious study and ritual. They speak it in pure form! This is even more remarkable when we recall the centuries, no millennia, of disuse and misuse. The Hebrew kept alive by the Yeshivas (schools) inevitably suffered in isolation. It fared no better elsewhere. By the late 1800s, the Jews left in Jerusalem spoke Yiddish, French or Arabic, not Hebrew. Even when Hebrew was required for intercommunication, Jewish people reverted to Medieval Hebrew, an outmoded and degraded version of the Biblical original. God had promised something far better.

"For at that time I will change the speech of the peoples to a pure speech, that all of them may call upon the name of the LORD and serve him with one accord." Zephaniah 3:9

The Lord used a resourceful man from Eastern Europe to accomplish this modern resurrection. Born Eliezer Perelman in Lithuania in 1858, Eliezer Ben-Yehuda caught the Zionist vision and emigrated to the Holy Land. He worked tirelessly to create a thoroughly modern Hebrew dictionary and to promote Hebrew as the language of instruction in schools. Sensing that this could never accomplish the goal, he and his wife, Deborah Jonas came up with a bold plan. Speaking only Hebrew in the home and isolating their family life from the outside, they brought up their son, Ben-Zion, as the first native speaking Hebrew child since the Diaspora began.

Now, *sabras* (native born Israelis) all speak Biblical Hebrew in a "pure" form, just as their God had promised so many years ago through His prophet Zephaniah. For those who have grown up with the reality of modern Israel, this may seem inconsequential. Oblivious to the facts, modern observers expect it as a matter of course that a nation would speak its ethnic tongue. Students of history and of prophecy, however, can see it for the astonishing miracle that it is. And move the minute hand on the Last Days clock just that much closer to the midnight hour…

3) The Restoration of the Jewish Nation

The nation of Israel was twice ruthlessly destroyed by the Romans—partially in 70-72 AD and completely in 130 AD. For almost two thousand years, the forlorn dream of Jews in exile from the land was to return to the land, if only as sojourners, dwelling inside another nation's territory. Few would have believed national restoration was possible. Then, first by the Zionist movement of the late 19th century and later by Nazi persecution, the Jewish people began returning to the Land in greater number. Meanwhile, the Treaty of Versailles in the aftermath of World War I assigned a portion of the Ottoman Empire as a future homeland for the Jews, placing Palestine under British protection for that very purpose.

The day that the British Mandate for Palestine expired, Israel's first Prime Minister, David Ben-Gurion, declared independence.

With the vote of the United Nations in its favor, Israel was reborn in a single day—May 14, 1948—just as the Lord prophesied through Isaiah. To top it off, Isaiah's exact words were fulfilled. Israel as a nation was "brought forth" and immediately afterward the "labor pains" of war began. The surrounding Islamic nations of Egypt, Jordan, Lebanon, Syria, Iraq, and Saudi Arabia all declared war the same day that Israel became a nation recognized by the world's governing authority. They failed to stop what God was doing through the valiant Jewish freedom-fighters.

"Before she was in labor she gave birth; before her pain came upon her she delivered a son. Who has heard such a thing? Who has seen such things? Shall a land be born in one day? Shall a nation be brought forth in one moment? For as soon as Zion was in labor she brought forth her children." Isaiah 66:7-8

Then say to them, Thus says the Lord God: Behold, I will take the people of Israel from the nations among which they have gone, and will gather them from all around, and bring them to their own land. And I will make them one nation in the land, on the mountains of Israel. Ezekiel 37:21

4) The Restoration of National Unity

Another marvel about the founding of Israel is one we might easily take for granted. The nation that emerged in 1948 was a united whole, a single nation. Well, that's normal isn't it? To this day, nations arise with a united purpose; only later might they splinter and divide. Indeed, division is exactly what happened to the nation of Israel under its third king, Solomon's heavy-handed son, Rehoboam. A disgruntled brother, Jeroboam, led the Northern Kingdom into rebellion against Judah and Benjamin in the south. That heart-breaking division remained right through the final destruction of Israel and the deportation of the ten northern tribes by Assyria in 722 BC.

When modern Israel declared its independence in 1948 no trace of that former division remained. Centuries of persecution during the Diaspora united the Jewish people with a shared dream of national restoration: "Next year in Jerusalem!" To be sure, political and religious differences of opinion abound in modern Israel, many with vehement intensity, but a common bond continues to hold the nation together. That common bond seems to have more to do with "us against the world" — the nations which seek their destruction — than with a shared faith in their national God. Nevertheless, this marvel of a united Israel was exactly predicted by Ezekiel over 2500 years ago.

Then say to them, Thus says the Lord God: Behold, I will take the people of Israel from the nations among which they have gone, and will gather them from all around, and bring them to their own land. And I will make them one nation in the land, on the mountains of Israel. And one king shall be king over them all, and they shall be no longer two nations, and no longer divided into two kingdoms. Ezekiel 37:21-22

5) Jerusalem and Israel in World Politics

Only a hundred and fifty years ago, who would have thought that Jerusalem could ever again have a role to play in world politics? Who could have conceived that it would become the very epi-center of global politics, a fault line setting the nations of the world in an uproar? The answer, of course, is no one except (perhaps) students of Bible prophecy. Even they must have been scratching their heads. Certainly, as shrewd an observer as Mark Twain didn't see it coming at all. Writing of his 1867 visit to the Holy Land, Twain marveled with undisguised scorn at the "romantic" accounts bandied about by religious tourists.

To find the sort of solitude to make one dreary come to Galilee for that... these unpeopled deserts, these rusty mounds of barrenness, that never, never, never do shake the glare from their harsh outlines... that melancholy ruin of Capernaum, this stupid village of Tiberias, slumbering under its six funereal palms... we never saw a human being on the whole route [to Tabor].
Mark Twain, *The Innocents Abroad*

Twain was hardly alone in his assessment. Others saw it too. Ten years earlier (in 1857) the British Consul in Palestine reported that the entire land was largely uninhabited, that its greatest need was repopulation. As late as 1895, French author Pierre Loti described a dismal scene: "As elsewhere, as everywhere in Palestine, city and palaces have returned to the dust... This melancholy of abandonment, weights on all of the Holy Land."[4] These men would be shocked and astonished by present events we largely take for granted. Their writings preserve for us an undeniable record of how stunningly and swiftly an Invisible Hand overthrew the old order: Exactly as it was prophesied!

A Continuing War Against the Jews

The mandate from heaven to regather the Jews and restore their nation flew in the face of newly discovered Saudi oil. All the leading nations of the world—especially in their covert operations—conspired against Israel's formation, including the United States. This sordid story has been masterfully chronicled by John Loftus and Mark Aarons in their book, *The Secret War Against the Jews*. Reading it, one is amazed that the Zionists were able to pull off their victory in the face of such intense international opposition. Indeed, only a great God could foretell it and accomplish it!

The average postwar citizen in the US and Europe wanted the Jews to have their homeland for the sake of the Holocaust. Nevertheless, powerful people in their governments were willing to sell out the Zionists to gain favor with the Saudis. As a matter of historic record, the first Saudi king, Ibn Saud, intensely hated Jews and vigorously resisted all efforts to restore them to their land. The deadly infection of hatred spread throughout Islam. Hence, from the 1930s on, a witches' brew of antisemitism, Arab oil and terrorist violence turned Jerusalem into a "cup of staggering" for the nations. Israel's emergence and survival are truly miraculous.

---

[4] Joan Peters, *From Time Immemorial* p. 161.

The oracle of the word of the Lord concerning Israel: Thus declares the Lord, who stretched out the heavens and founded the earth and formed the spirit of man within him: "Behold, I am about to make Jerusalem a cup of staggering to all the surrounding peoples. The siege of Jerusalem will also be against Judah. On that day I will make Jerusalem a heavy stone for all the peoples. All who lift it will surely hurt themselves. And all the nations of the earth will gather against it. Zechariah 12:1-4

Positioned to See Him

This miraculous Jewish sign is all the more compelling because Zechariah linked it to the ultimate realization by the Jews that Jesus is their Messiah. This Jewish nation, surrounded by enemies and at the center of world events, would see "him whom they have pierced." Present day Israel will see Jesus return and "weep bitterly" to behold that He is the Messiah they rejected. This prophecy gives us a highly focused sign of the nearness of our Lord's Return. Israel not only had to be reborn for this to take place—for them to be in position to "look on" Him. It also had to become "a cup of staggering" from earlier in the same chapter. We are there!

"And I will pour out on the house of David and the inhabitants of Jerusalem a spirit of grace and pleas for mercy, so that, when they look on me, on him whom they have pierced, they shall mourn for him, as one mourns for an only child, and weep bitterly over him, as one weeps over a firstborn." Zechariah 12:10

6) The Conversion of the Jews

Previous centuries have seen both forced Jewish converts to Christianity who practiced their Jewish faith secretly and willing, believing converts who were then assimilated into Gentile Christianity. With the fall of Jerusalem and the Diaspora of the first century, Gentile Christianity has been the only game in town.

Something new arrived only recently on the scene: Jews who retain their Jewish heritage and identity when coming to faith in Christ. The rise of Messianic Jews in the past few decades marks a shift towards the end of the age of the Gentiles. For more on this, see "Gospel Signs of Jesus' Return" coming up in the next article.

This Story Is Not Over

Many more prophecies regarding the Jews remain to be fulfilled. And they will be. Tragically, however, not all the future events will be as positive as those which have already occurred. Unbridled persecution, catastrophic wars, and massive relocations are yet to come. By the time we see those signs, the last of the Last Days will be mercifully nearing the end. We have been given these signs in advance so that we can know—know with an absolute certainty—that we have already entered days the prophets foresaw. Without a doubt we are living in the days immediately before Messiah's Return.

THREE GOSPEL SIGNS

Peter foresaw that the return of the Lord Jesus would be significantly delayed. He saw, too, that this unexpectedly long delay would give scoffers additional reason for doubting that Jesus would come back at all. It might even cause sincere believers to question this epic promise of the Lord. According, he gives us two important insights into the timing of the Second Coming.

Knowing this first of all, that scoffers will come in the last days with scoffing, following their own sinful desires. They will say, "Where is the promise of his coming? For ever since the fathers fell asleep, all things are continuing as they were from the beginning of creation." ... But do not overlook this one fact, beloved, that with the Lord one day is as a thousand years, and a thousand years as one day. The Lord is not slow to fulfill his promise as some count slowness, but is patient toward you, not wishing that any should perish, but that all should reach repentance. 2 Peter 3:3-4, 8-9

We who are enmeshed in time easily "overlook" the reality that God isn't. Because God is outside our time and space, His view of time's passage is radically different from ours. For Him, a thousand years is as one day. That Jesus said He was coming back "soon" just doesn't sound the same to His ears as it does to ours! However, there is a further mystery here that is well worth exploring. It is the "Sign of the Seventh Year" and it relates directly to the timeline of the Lord's Return.[5] Jesus and the Father have been laboring to accomplish humanity's redemption for six thousand years, or six days by Their reckoning. Their day of rest is close at hand—the thousand year Millennium of Christ's reign.

---

[5] Refer to *Signs of the Last Days* by this author at Amazon or read the article posted at https://www.thelastdays.info/signs/sign-of-the-seventh

The Father's Heart of Love

By far the more endearing reason for the delay is the Father's Heart. Jesus told us, "God so loves the world" that He doesn't want anyone to be lost. Grace shows up here as God's gift of time—time that allows everyone the chance to repent. Well, "OK," the Early Church may have said. "Give us a generation to get the message out. That's all the time we'll need." To their understanding the world was largely confined to the Mediterranean Basin—well within their reach. They had no practical concept of the immense size of the earth, or that it was already covered by far-flung nations entirely unknown to them. Ah, but not unknown to our Father!

That's why the long delay makes perfect sense. The gospel must go out to the whole world, not just the ones who first received it. That kind of universal evangelism was a practical impossibility before the invention of modern means of transport. Interestingly, this unavoidable delay on our part in reaching all the way around the world, would give God even more time to bring "many sons and daughters to glory."[6] Just consider this: by some accounts, the population of the world *then* was about 300 million. Now it is over seven billion. Our God is after an immense harvest! Many signs are saying the time is ripe for the greatest in-gathering of souls the world has ever seen.

1) The Gospel to the World

For the first time in world history, the gospel is on the verge of reaching every living person. This is all the more amazing since the numbers are increasing exponentially. By the time Jesus returns there may well be more Christians alive on the earth, than have ever lived. However, as quickly as the world's population has grown in recent years, technology has grown even more swiftly. New means of electronic communication have brushed aside all former limits to reaching the world.

Consider the different paths which are converging now. The "old school" method for reaching the lost required years of training

---

[6] Hebrews 2:10 NIV

for missionaries and Bible translators alike. They often sowed their entire lives into missionary work overseas. This work progressed painstakingly slowly, but it is now reaching its zenith. The Bible is at last being targeted for translation into every known language. The gospel is also being carried by missionaries into every known people group as a witness to all the nations. This monumental task is nearly completed.

Old School Meets New Tech

At the same time, recent developments have flooded the entire planet with astonishing new high-tech capacities to spread the gospel. The internet, satellite television, radio and cell phones span the globe, bringing the message of salvation into the very air surrounding every tribe and nation. Which will get the job done first? Probably, the answer is both! There is no way, however, for us to decide the issue. We don't even know when one individual has fairly and fully "heard" the gospel, let alone seven billion. But we are clearly getting close. All of this had to happen first, then the end can come. Can anyone dispute that it is happening?

As he sat on the Mount of Olives, the disciples came to him privately, saying, "Tell us, when will these things be, and what will be the sign of your coming and of the close of the age?" And Jesus answered them, "...And this gospel of the kingdom will be proclaimed throughout the whole world as a testimony to all nations, and then the end will come. Matthew 24:3-5,14

2) The Tabernacle of David

For the church as a whole, there is a little-known sign that has, perhaps, escaped the attention of many. Of course, it is well-known to those who are involved in it, but this is still a remnant portion compared to the whole. This gospel sign is the emergence of a worldwide prayer and praise movement. Prayer and praise that is offered before the Lord as continuous worship is prophesied of the end of the age.

In that day will I raise up the tabernacle of David that is fallen, and close up the breaches thereof; and I will raise up its ruins, and I will build it as in the days of old. Amos 9:11 ASV

"After this I will return, and I will rebuild the tent of David that has fallen; I will rebuild its ruins, and I will restore it, that the remnant of mankind may seek the Lord, and all the Gentiles who are called by my name, says the Lord, who makes these things known from of old." Acts 15:16-17

King David commissioned a sizable troop of worshippers and musicians to offer continuous prayer and praise at the Tabernacle in Jerusalem. Except for the century-long 24/7 prayer vigil of the Moravians at Herrnhut in Germany, the earth has rarely seen such extravagant worship sustained on the Davidic scale. Curiously, this too, is one of the things God is raising up in the earth today and restoring to the life of the church. A 24/7 worship and intercessory movement began in Kansas City, Missouri in 1999. According to founding pastor Mike Bickle, The International House of Prayer (IHOP) has inspired a hundred other prayer groups all over the world to follow their lead.

3) Messianic Jewish Believers

A long-awaited sign is finally coming to pass. The conversion of Jews at the end of the age of the Gentiles is a present reality. Previous centuries have seen forced Jewish converts to Christianity who continued to practice their Jewish faith secretly. Willing, believing converts—though rare—had no other option than to be assimilated into Gentile Christianity with a resulting loss of their Jewish heritage. Such Jewish conversions were in themselves proof that the "age of the Gentiles" was still in full swing.

Something radically different is happening in our day. Messianic Jewish congregation can be found in most major cities and even small communities. These are Jewish converts to Christian faith in Jesus, but who retain their Jewish heritage and identity. They keep the Jewish festivals, their congregations are presided over by Rabbis, yet they enthusiastically worship Jesus as their Messiah. This phenomenon has not been seen on earth since the expulsion of Jewish Christians from the synagogues late in the first century following the destruction of the Temple in Jerusalem. Messianic Judaism began in the 1960s and has been growing rapidly ever since. It marks a dramatic shift towards the end of the age of the Gentiles.

And even they, if they do not continue in their unbelief, will be grafted in, for God has the power to graft them in again. For if you were cut from what is by nature a wild olive tree, and grafted, contrary to nature, into a cultivated olive tree, how much more will these, the natural branches, be grafted back into their own olive tree. Lest you be wise in your own sight, I do not want you to be unaware of this mystery, brothers: a partial hardening has come upon Israel, until the fullness of the Gentiles has come in. Romans 11:23-25

They will fall by the edge of the sword and be led captive among all nations, and Jerusalem will be trampled underfoot by the Gentiles, until the times of the Gentiles are fulfilled. Luke 21:24

Who Can Argue with these Signs?

These gospel signs are utterly unprecedented. Until this generation the gospel clearly had not reached the entire world. Now, it is covering the globe. Prior to 1999, continuous prayer and praise simply didn't exist. It has been going on non-stop ever since then and will continue to blossom. Only a half century ago, the phrase "messianic Jew" or "completed Jew" was unheard of. Now, the emergence of Jewish converts on a large scale and of a fully Jewish character is bringing down the curtain on the exclusive faith-hold of Gentile Christianity itself. These signs are not only unprecedented, they are incontrovertible. Who can possibly argue that Biblical prophecies of the Last Days are not being dramatically fulfilled in our day?

FIVE GLOBAL SIGNS

The Book of Revelation gives us a picture of the whole world organized against God along with signs of global deterioration. These are completely unprecedented Biblical signs that simply were not happening until the middle of the 20th century. In our day, they are an avalanche carrying us into the Last Days.

1) Environmental Signs

We now have the capacity to destroy the environment. All by ourselves we can kill life in the rivers and aquifers (springs of water); kill one third of the life in the ocean (with oil spills or worse); cause ourselves to be scorched by the sun (with the loss of the ozone layer); and spread plagues world-wide in a matter of hours (jet travel). This means that humanity has "gained" the ability to bring catastrophic calamities upon ourselves and the entire earth. This has never happened before. Our destructive powers were limited to local disasters due to our limited technological ability. Notice how these newly acquired abilities dovetail with prophetic passages from the Book of Revelation.

The second angel poured out his bowl into the sea, and it became like the blood of a corpse, and every living thing died that was in the sea. The third angel poured out his bowl into the rivers and the springs of water, and they became blood. Revelation 16:3-4

The fourth angel poured out his bowl on the sun, and it was allowed to scorch people with fire. They were scorched by the fierce heat, and they cursed the name of God who had power over these plagues. They did not repent and give him glory. Revelation 16:8-9

An Unwitting Instrument of Judgment

It must be said that God doesn't need our help when it comes to judging us. The Almighty is perfectly able to do things on His own, as the above passages seem to indicate. Angels sound the trumpets or pour the bowls and calamities happen. So, it hardly matters that we have "matching" destructive abilities. The Last Days judgments could happen without any human agency involved—just as it was with Sodom and Gomorrah. Nevertheless, in the Old Testament the Lord frequently used one nation to be the instrument of inflicting His judgment upon another. This was indeed the more frequent manner, as any reading through the major and minor prophets immediately confirms. It is, therefore, an extraordinary sign that we are now in the position of becoming an instrument for rendering judgment upon ourselves. It doesn't have to happen that way, but is it not (at least) both bizarre and deeply troubling that it could?

2) Political and Economic Signs

We now have a one world financial system. Babylon as it is pictured in the Book of Revelation looks like world capitalism corrupted by unrestrained greed. How did we get here? The history of western expansion since the Middle Ages shows that wherever commercial trade went, governmental authority followed, since safe-guarding trade required treaties. Trade treaties in turn led to military interventions to enforce them, because laws are powerless without "the sword." The conquest of India by the British and the Opium War they waged against China are outstanding examples of trade connections leading to power structures. This greed-corrupted side of commerce will come under judgment, perhaps sooner than we think.

After this I saw another angel coming down from heaven, having great authority, and the earth was made bright with his glory. And he called out with a mighty voice, "Fallen, fallen is Babylon the great! ... and the merchants of the earth have grown rich from the power of her luxurious living." Revelation 18:1-3

World War II brought the nations of the world together in total war on an unparalleled scale. Its aftermath left the belligerent nations united in mutual interdependence through banking, industry, and commerce. It also left many grieving souls yearning to see a world without war. Out of the chaos, the United Nations emerged along with the World Bank, the World Court, and (naturally enough) the UN's police force. We now have a one-world government. Although it is still in its infancy, it is inevitably growing towards centralization of power and despotic control, just as the world-wide economy is hastening towards irreversible interdependence.

The Dark Side of Globalization

The one-world economic system is several steps ahead of the one-world governmental system. Real authority for the world governing bodies is more *de jure*, than *de facto*. We can be sure, however, that there are powerful people who are helping globalization along. Some see it as the proper evolution of society necessary for the survival of humanity. Others see it as an opportunity for their own autocratic control over the world's wealth and inhabitants. We already know that this dark side will seize control with the rise of the antichrist. Signs abound that this "beast system" is already in full preparation mode.

And they worshiped the dragon who gave authority to the beast. And they worshiped the beast, saying, Who is like the beast? Who is able to make war with it? And a mouth speaking great things was given to it, and blasphemies. And authority was given to it to continue forty-two months. Revelation 13:4-5 MKJV

Efforts continue at developing a one-world religious system, also prophesied in Revelation. There are compelling signs that this could take place through the Vatican and its present vicar, Pope Francis. Like many events of this century, the formation of the second beast's religious system may happen swiftly, even more swiftly than the one-world order for government. Taken together, these are unprecedented global signs clearly envisioned in the Book of Revelation of what the world would be like in the Last Days.

3) Technological Signs

The mark of the beast is easily the most talked about sign of the Last Days. It has been so for years. When I was young—back in the sixties—none of us in Christian youth fellowship could imagine why anyone would want to take such an obviously evil sign. And what would it be? Was it a tattoo? How crude! Then, bar codes came out. Now we have it! The unfolding reality is more subtle and ingenious—from the standpoint of serving the Evil One's purpose.

We now have the technological ability to put a mark (a smart chip) under the skin of the hand or the forehead. Ultimately, no buying or selling can be done without that mark. That's the final, compulsory reason for taking the chip. But what will gain it favor in the beginning? The answer is identity theft. None of us saw that coming either. Identity theft was unheard of until the electronic age. Now, all of us can see in the chip a rationale for ensuring safe and secure transactions. Few of us—the Christian few—will see beyond the chip to realize that it is the forbidden mark.

Also it causes all, both small and great, both rich and poor, both free and slave, to be marked on the right hand or the forehead, so that no one can buy or sell unless he has the mark, that is, the name of the beast or the number of its name. This calls for wisdom: let the one who has understanding calculate the number of the beast, for it is the number of a man, and his number is 666. Revelation 13:16-18

A Living, Breathing Image

Technology also ushered in another strange twist. In the sixties the idea of a speaking image of the beast could barely be imagined. We had posters of dictators and grainy images of Hitler on film, but it took Hollywood to lead the way. Well in advance of real technology, science fiction and special effects began bringing speaking, holographic images right before our eyes. Now, it is easy to "see" how the second beast could bring the antichrist's image visibly to "life" all over the planet. Add to human ingenuity and creativity, supernatural enhancements provided by spiritual darkness and you have something only John the Revelator could have seen coming!

And by the signs that it is allowed to work in the presence of the beast it deceives those who dwell on earth, telling them to make an image for the beast that was wounded by the sword and yet lived. And it was allowed to give breath to the image of the beast, so that the image of the beast might even speak and might cause those who would not worship the image of the beast to be slain. Revelation 13:14-15

4) Persecution of Christians

In the West until recently, we tended to think of Christian martyrdom as a thing of the past—a tragic oddity that mercifully ended when the Roman Empire converted to Christianity in the 4th Century. Sure, there were wars of religion that bloodied Europe in the wake of the Protestant Reformation. But that was Christians killing Christians. Our idea of martyrdom was covered with the dust of history. Christian believers in China and elsewhere knew better, of course, but the western Church largely fell asleep.

The sudden rise of Isis (the Islamic State) changed that gross misperception. Now we know that Christians are indeed being killed in our own day. Perversely, Christians are not only being martyred, they are actually being beheaded. We are even seeing evidence of this atavistic practice with our own eyes. This is a double confirmation of ancient prophecy! Who would ever have thought that beheadings would make a gruesome return to public view? Yet, all this was foreseen by John on Patmos.

Also I saw the souls of those who had been beheaded for the testimony of Jesus and for the word of God, and those who had not worshiped the beast or its image and had not received

its mark on their foreheads or their hands. They came to life and reigned with Christ for a thousand years. Revelation 20:4

Martyrdom on the Rise

What may still not be widely known is that martyrdom had already been dramatically on the increase long before the rise of militant Islam. The number of Christians that have been killed in the last 100 years exceeds the total from the previous 1900 years. Millions of Christians were killed by Hitler. Millions more were murdered by the communist regimes of Stalin, Mao Zedong and other "enlightened" atheists. It's not just politicians; it is also religious fanatics who persecute Christians. Believers in Jesus to this day suffer death at the hands of radical Hindus and Buddhists, not to mention Satanists. All of this was prophesied two thousand years ago.

Then they were each given a white robe and told to rest a little longer, until the number of their fellow servants and their brothers should be complete, who were to be killed as they themselves had been. Revelation 6:11

Sadly, it is not over. We should all be prepared to face the looming persecution and—by God's grace and strength—face down all fear any fear we may have of it. According to the Book of Revelation, many Christians will die during the Great Tribulation as martyrs. It will be their ultimate act of courage and devotion offered to the Lord in the most trying of times. These will "escape" the other horrors of the Tribulation and receive one of the highest honors of heaven, a martyr's crown.

Then one of the elders addressed me, saying, "Who are these, clothed in white robes, and from where have they come?" I said to him, "Sir, you know." And he said to me, "These are the ones coming out of the great tribulation. They have washed their robes and made them white in the blood of the Lamb. "Therefore they are before the throne of God, and serve him

**day and night in his temple; and he who sits on the throne
will shelter them with his presence.** Revelation 7:13-15

An Unthinkable Reversal

Fifty years ago, a world-wide persecution of Christians seemed
unthinkable, fantastic. Christianity throughout the West was a
major part of the glue that held civilization together. Christians and
Christian leaders enjoyed a favorable position on the world's stage.
Christian morality was still held in honor. All that is rapidly
changing. We did not know then that what would replace the
hegemony of Christian values was not something non-Christian,
which may have been benign, but a far darker thing of active
menace.

The once-Christian lands, in moving away from Christ, are now
becoming anti-Christ. Already the Name that is above all names
can hardly be mentioned in the public square anywhere in the
West. Worse, those who pursue alternative lifestyles view His
scriptures as their sworn enemy. Those who believe the scriptures
are vilified. This is one of the greatest "woes" spoken of by Isaiah.
When evil is called good, good becomes evil.[7] Wherever these "anti-
Christians" come into political power, Christians are hounded and
harassed. Soon they could be martyred. The entire world is filling
out the picture of persecution painted in the Book of Revelation.

5) The Information Age

One predicted sign of the Last Days is something that we all
enjoy: the internet. Another sign just as enthusiastically pursed is
world travel, whether for business or pleasure. Remarkably, Daniel
foresaw both. As brilliant as Daniel was, there was no way he could
have seen this coming by his own understanding. No, our present
age of information and jet travel is an absolute confirmation that
Daniel received genuine prophetic visions. God alone can see our
future more clearly than we do our present. At the end of the
vision, the angel told Daniel to seal up the prophecies he was

---

[7] Isaiah 5:20

shown until a time when knowledge would increase as well as travel. Since both are happening now, we can also expect that the Lord will soon be unsealing things that are still hidden in scripture about the Last Days.

"But you, Daniel, shut up the words and seal the book, until the time of the end. Many shall run to and fro, and knowledge shall increase." Daniel 12:4

Putting It All Together

What can we say to these things? These global signs alone make an irrefutable case for the timeline of Last Days prophecies in the Bible. Without question these signs have all been falling into place over the last fifty years. Equally without question, none of them were even visible on the horizon one hundred years ago—except for those few with scripture enhanced vision. Whether the signs are environmental, economic, political, or technological; whether they have to do with an increased persecution of Christians, or with the increase of information and travel—they all point dramatically to these being the days just prior to Jesus' Return. Let's be sure to get ready!

APPENDIX A

Endnotes

He who testifies to these things says,
"Surely I am coming soon."
Amen. Come, Lord Jesus!

Revelation 22:21

APPENDIX A

ENDNOTES

Chapter 2: The Visitation at Patmos

[1] Cambridge Dictionary defines speculation as "the act of guessing possible answers to a question without having enough information to be certain." It derives from the Latin word "speculari" which means "to look at, view, observe" and originally indicated "close observation and intelligent contemplation." By the late 1500s it gained the disparaging sense it carries today of "mere conjecture." See etymonline.com.
[2] Adam is the type; Jesus, the "second Adam" is the antitype: Romans 5:14
[3] See Matthew 28:16-20 and Mark 16:14-16.
[4] Acts 15:20, Acts 15:29 and Acts 21:25.
[5] Read Chapter 2 carefully. Though there is scholarly debate around it, this seems to be describing exactly the kind of problem that the Jerusalem Council letter sought to resolve.
[6] Acts 15:30-31
[7] Mark 13:32
[8] 1 John 4:1-3
[9] Revelation 22:8-9
[10] Hebrews 1:14
[11] Hebrews 2:6-7
[12] 2 Timothy 4:8
[13] John 1:1
[14] Matthew 17:2
[15] Psalm 60:5
[16] Hebrews 7:16
[17] Acts 2:24
[18] 1 Corinthians 13:12

Chapter 3: The First Church: Ephesus

[1] Genesis 25:33-34
[2] Ecclesiastes 3:11
[3] The Book of Enoch identifies some angelic beings as "Watchers"—a name which indicates their ordained role in watching over an assigned group. We also know that angels are "ministering spirits" to individuals: Hebrews 1:14
[4] Revelation 1:20
[5] Romans 2:11; Acts 10:34
[6] Psalm 60:5
[7] Hebrews 13:20
[8] Job 1:7
[9] 1 Peter 5:8

10 Matthew 10:42

11 Isaiah 64:6 KJV

12 Scholars generally believe that John's letters were written between 85-100 AD—a timeframe that would on average pre-date the Revelation which was penned just prior to 96 AD: 1 John 4:1

13 This calling comes after Jacob was restored to his brother Esau and was settled back in the Land. It is a calling to draw near and worship God now that he is in the Land: Genesis 35:1 See the whole chapter for the rest of the story.

14 1 Corinthians 13:3.

15 2 Timothy 2:24-26

16 I will not try to look up and list all of them I've read. One stands head and shoulders above the rest: Francois Fenelon, Archbishop of Cambrai and defender of Madame Guyon. Get anything by him you can. He lived during the time of the Sun King in France. The Queen of Poland said of him that although others proved the truth of faith, "Fenelon taught us to love it."

17 As the disciples on the road to Emmaus recalled of their encounter with Jesus: They said to each other, "Did not our hearts burn within us while he talked to us on the road, while he opened to us the Scriptures?" Luke 24:32

18 John 6:28-29

19 Matthew 5:15-16

20 Psalm 139:21-22

21 This is spoken to Saul, but it references David as the prince chosen to replace him: 1 Samuel 13:14

22 Now the Spirit expressly says that in later times some will depart from the faith by devoting themselves to deceitful spirits and teachings of demons, through the insincerity of liars whose consciences are seared, who forbid marriage and require abstinence from foods [the KJV rendering of "meats" here is more accurate] that God created to be received with thanksgiving by those who believe and know the truth. For everything created by God is good, and nothing is to be rejected if it is received with thanksgiving. 1 Timothy 4:1-4

23 Ephesians 19:27-28

24 See https://www.thattheworldmayknow.com/artemis-of-the-ephesians

25 Matthew 6:24 KJV; 1 John 2:15

Chapter 4: The Second Church: Smyrna

1 Jesus is the living Word, the "mouth of God," ever speaking life-giving truths to His people: Deuteronomy 8:3

2 https://www.britannica.com/place/Izmir

3 Daniel 3:8

4 See The First Church: Ephesus, pp 34-35

5 Hebrews 12:1-2 MKJV

6. John 16:2

7 Romans 8:1

8 Isaiah 54:17

9 Ephesians 3:8

10 1 Corinthians 10:13

[11] 2 Corinthians 4:17-18

[12] "The Five Crowns, also known as the Five Heavenly Crowns, is a concept in Christian theology that pertains to the five crowns that individuals can receive after the Last Judgment. These are the Crown of Life, the Incorruptible Crown, the Crown of Righteousness, the Crown of Glory, and the Crown of Exultation." Source: https://en.wikipedia.org/wiki/Five_crowns

[13] Revelation 4:10-11

[14] Romans 10:17

[15] Romans 16:20

[16] Hebrews 9:27 MKJV

Chapter 5: The Third Church: Pergamum

[1] Britannica online encyclopedia: https://www.britannica.com/place/Pergamum

[2] See The First Church: Ephesus, pp 34-35

[3] Peter warns against being showing the angelic beings any dishonor with this example: 2 Peter 2:11-12

[4] Romans 13:3-4

[5] Hebrews 4:12-13

[6] 2 Corinthians 4:3-4

[7] Ephesians 2:2; Ephesians 6:12

[8] http://cfi-usa.org/pergamon-to-berlin/

[9] I Corinthians 10:19-20

[10] https://en.wikipedia.org/wiki/Blood_and_Iron_%28speech%29 Germany's Chancellor Bismarck's famous speech in 1800s.

[11] Job 1:7

[12] Numbers 31:16

[13] Numbers 25:1-2

[14] Exodus 34:6

[15] John 16:12

[16] 2 Corinthians 5:17

[17] Colossians 3:3

[18] 1 John 3:2

Chapter 6: The Fourth Church: Thyatira

[1] I Kings 21:23, 25-26

[2] See The First Church: Ephesus, pp 34-35

[3] John 14:12

[4] Haggai 2:9

[5] Luke 22:44

[6] Romans 8:37

Chapter 7: The Fifth Church: Sardis

[1] https://www.britannica.com/place/Sardis

[2] Ecclesiastes 11:1

³ It was protocol for wedding garments to be made available for guests at royal feasts in the ancient Middle East (See 2 Kings 10:22.

[3] It was protocol for wedding garments to be made available for guests at royal feasts in the ancient Middle East (See 2 Kings 10:22.
[4] Revelation 19:7-9
[5] See The First Church: Ephesus, pp 34-35
[6] The seven spirits are manifestations of the Holy Spirit. We are given the number of them by Jesus to John. Their description (in part) was given to Isaiah: And the Spirit of the LORD [Holy Spirit] shall rest upon him [Messiah Jesus], the Spirit of wisdom and understanding, the Spirit of counsel and might, the Spirit of knowledge and the fear of the LORD. And his delight shall be in the fear of the LORD. He shall not judge by what his eyes see, or decide disputes by what his ears hear. Isaiah 11:2-3 [bracket portions added]
[7] 1 John 4:18-19
[8] John 15:5
[9] Luke 10:41-42
[10] Jeremiah 33:11
[11] 1 Kings 19:18
[12] 2 Corinthians 2:14
[13] 1 John 5:4

Chapter 8: The Sixth Church: Philadelphia

[1] https://en.wikipedia.org/wiki/Ala%C5%9Fehir
[2] Acts 9:1-2
[3] Acts 9:4-5
[4] Acts 17:6
[5] Philippians 3:5-6
[6] Romans 10:2-3
[7] See The First Church: Ephesus, pp 34-35
[8] Matthew 18:20
[9] 1 Thessalonians 5:11
[10] Romans 10:13
[11] John 16:2
[12] Romans 2:28-29
[13] Philippians 3:3
[14] Acts 9:4-5
[15] John 16:2
[16] Isaiah 55:8
[17] 1 Corinthians 13:13
[18] Hebrews 1:3-4
[19] Hebrews 2:7-8
[20] Galatians 4:26

Chapter 9: The Seventh Church: Laodicea

[1] https://www.britannica.com/place/Laodicea
[2] Philippians 2:12-13
[3] 2 Thessalonians 2:13

[4] See The First Church: Ephesus, pp 34-35

[5] Ecclesiastes 7:5

[6] The verb form occurs more than one hundred times in the Old Testament and means to take care, to be faithful, reliable or established, or to believe someone or something. The idea of something that is faithful, reliable, or believable seems to lie behind the use of amen as an exclamation on twenty-five solemn occasions in the Old Testament. https://www.biblestudytools.com/dictionary/amen/

[7] John 18:37

[8] John 1:1-3

[9] Matthew 25:23

[10] Philippians 3:14

[11] Matthew 6:19-20

[12] John 3:5

[13] Romans 14:17

APPENDIX B

The Matthew 24 Timeline

*"From the fig tree learn its lesson:
as soon as its branch becomes tender and puts out its leaves,
you know that summer is near.
So also, when you see these things taking place,
you know that he [the Son of Man] is near,
at the very gates."*

Mark 13:28-29

THE MATTHEW 24 TIMELINE

Did Jesus give us a timeline for the major events of the End Times? Yes, He did! This wonderful timeline includes the Birth Pains, the Great Tribulation, the rise of the antichrist and all the stunning events of His Return. It functions like a skeleton, providing the structural element that supports living flesh and connects it the right way. The only thing left for us to do is to "put meat on these bones" by taking other End Times passages from elsewhere in the Bible and attach them at the right spot. Of course, if you take this skeleton apart and rearrange it (as some do), you don't get a lovely prophetic creation from Jesus, you get a monstrosity. But why would anyone want to do that? Especially, when Jesus has already told us what we need to know.

Jesus answered him, "I have spoken openly to the world. I have always taught in synagogues and in the temple, where all Jews come together. I have said nothing in secret. John 18:20

The Matthew 24 Timeline

This timeline—usually called the "Olivet Discourse"—came forth not as prepared remarks during class time, but simply in the course of an ordinary conversation. Of course, nothing with Jesus is ordinary. The disciples found that out when they came to Jesus wanting to share the view with Him of the temple's buildings as they were departing from its grounds.

1. Jesus Predicts the Temple's Destruction

And Jesus went out and departed from the temple. And His disciples came to Him to show Him the buildings of the temple. And Jesus said to them, Do you not see all these things? Truly I say to you, There shall not be left here one stone on another that shall not be thrown down. Matthew 24:1-2 MKJV

Coming from the sticks (Galilee), the disciples would have been over-awed by the splendor and magnificence of Herod's temple in Jerusalem. They expected Jesus to join with them in praising it. Instead, He shattered their mood by foretelling its utter destruction. There would not be even "one stone on another that shall not be thrown down." The arrow went deep. The Temple stood for something far greater and more substantial than itself. It could only be thrown down, if God were to bring a terrible judgment against the Jewish nation.

The Lord would never do that unless an equally frightful event occurred—the falling away of Israel into apostacy and idolatry. Jesus' words touched a nerve. Just such a dread national calamity had already occurred six hundred years earlier resulting in Nebuchadnezzar's destruction of Solomon's Temple. Could it happen again? Is it any wonder that the disciples peppered Jesus with a flurry of questions?

2. The Disciples Ask Three Questions

And as He sat on the Mount of Olives, the disciples came to Him privately, saying, Tell us, when shall these things be? And what shall be the sign of Your coming, and of the end of the world? Matthew 24:3 MKJV

Upon descending the temple mount, Jesus and His disciples would have crossed the lush and lovely Kidron Valley with its tombs of the kings and the Garden of Gethsemane, then climbed to the crest of the Mount of Olives. All Jerusalem lay before their gaze, but the only thing that held their attention for that half hour walk was the sobering effect of Jesus' words. As soon as their Master was seated, they approached Him with the question filling their minds (and ours).

What they asked was not one, but three separate questions. When will the temple be destroyed? What will be the sign of Your Return? And, what will be the sign of the "end of the world"? Jesus bypassed the first question ("when will these things be"—the temple's destruction) and dealt with the other two. Curiously, that first question would have been the one of most immediate concern to the disciples since it would occur in their lifetime. Yet, He passed over it in favor of giving them what is of far greater interest to us—the events that will likely happen in our lifetime. What He gives us through them are signs of the moment of His return ("Your coming") and of the final days of this present age of grace ("the end of the world").

Pause here for a second: How did they know Jesus would be leaving and then coming back? Remember, they were unable to receive or believe any of His words about His death and resurrection, yet here they reveal an expectation that Jesus would be returning. The Jewish people fully expected their Messiah to come at the end of the age and set right all things that were wrong (i.e. the other nations). Apparently, the disciples could read the signs of their day well enough to know that they weren't living in the prophesied end times. Even so, they had a slender grasp of the Jesus' divine purpose in coming in this in-between time.

3. Jesus Warns against Deception

And Jesus answered and said to them, Take heed that no man deceive you. For many will come in My name, saying, I am Christ, and will deceive many. And you will hear of wars and rumors of wars. See that you are not troubled, for all these things must occur; but the end is not yet. Matthew 24:4-6 MKJV

Jesus began with a stern warning. We need to hear it, too—and heed it as if our lives depend upon it. The thing of first importance our Lord evidently wants us to know is that these will be extremely deceptive times. There will be false messiahs and false messages. "Many" will be deceived by this. Let's remember that the word *Christ* or *messiah* in Jesus' day was not a man's name, but a title that meant a heaven-sent savior. Many will claim to be able to "save" humanity from the troubles coming on the earth. That's the thing to watch out for. There will also be wars and "rumors" of even more wars breaking out (think nightly news). We are not to be "troubled" by such reports, deceived into thinking that they are signs that the world is about to end. These things are unavoidable, but "the end is not yet." Other things have to happen first.

4. The Beginning of Sorrows (Birth Pains)

For nation will rise against nation, and kingdom against kingdom. And there will be famines and pestilences and earthquakes in different places. All these are the beginning of sorrows. Matthew 24:7-8 MKJV

Now, Jesus describes conditions which He calls "the beginning of sorrows," a phrase which carries the meaning of the pains or throes (travail) of childbirth.[1] Hence, these pre-tribulation "sorrows" are often referred to as "birth pains" or "pangs" (from the old KJV). The picture here is of a world going into the convulsions of labor as the new thing God is doing is birthed upon the earth. As with human birth pains, we can expect an increase in magnitude (of the pain they will inflict) and in frequency, as these "contractions" come closer together.

Specifically, we are to watch for famines, pestilences (plagues) and earthquakes world-wide. These calamities are already increasing. In addition, the fabric of human society will be torn as nation (ethnic group) rises against ethnic group and kingdoms (what we would call nations) rise against kingdoms. This sign, too, is falling into place. Although we do not have a world war going on, the number of wars worldwide is rising sharply.

5. Tribulation and Persecution Begin

Then they will deliver you up to be afflicted [this also can be translated as "tribulation" and "persecution"] and will kill you. And you will be hated of all nations for My name's sake. And then many will be offended, and will betray one another, and will hate one another. And many false prophets will rise and

---

[1] From Strong's Complete Concordance: *odin* Akin to G3601; a pang or throe, especially of childbirth: - pain, sorrow, travail.

deceive many. And because iniquity shall abound, the love of many will become cold. Matthew 24:9-12 MKJV

Once the birth pains reach a certain level, worldwide persecution of Christians will break out. We are not given an exact moment in time to watch for, but this shift to universal "hatred" will likely mark the beginning of the "Great" Tribulation. Jesus does not say if the two events (birth pains and persecution) are causally related, though it may be that Christians and Jews will be blamed for the calamities striking the earth. Nor is He saying that there will be no persecution until this time.

Jesus is the One who stated plainly that "in the world" we would "have tribulation."[2] The word He used (translated here as "afflicted") includes the meaning of persecution and indeed, times of persecution have always plagued the church. However, during this time we "will be hated of *all* nations." This is a worldwide persecution as unbelievers turn against the Church at some point during the season of "sorrows" He described initially.

This will prove too much for some believers to bear. Verses 10 to 12 heartbreakingly describe not unbelievers, but Christians turning against Christians. We can expect betrayals as "many" believers become "offended," forsaking the true faith and denouncing those who keep it.[3] Only those Christians who understand and believe the Biblical prophetic narrative will be in step with the Lord during this time of great distress. Apparently, other believers will be deceived by the worldview of the world around them--and think that the Last Days remnant Bride is the problem.

Deception will increase, so much so, that lawlessness "will abound" even among believers. For many people of faith, the love of God and love of man will simply "grow cold" as their

---

[2] John 16:33

[3] Strongs: The word for offended is *skandalizo* which means to "scandalize"; from G4625; to entrap, that is, trip up (figuratively stumble [transitively] or entice to sin, apostasy or displeasure): - (make to) offend.

faith dies. Knowing this possibility exists, pray that it never happens to you or yours. Jesus is warning us so we can prepare.

6. Perseverance, Dedication and Blessing

But he who endures to the end, the same shall be kept safe. And this gospel of the kingdom shall be proclaimed in all the world as a witness to all nations. And then the end shall come. Matthew 24:13-14 MKJV

The conditions in the previous verses lead into a glorious promise that contains a warning. Jesus promises that help will come to those "who endure to the end." Those who set their "hearts on pilgrimage" to pass faithfully through these perilous times are guaranteed that God will keep them safe.[4] Does this mean no physical harm will come their way? Hardly. Jesus previously declared that many faithful believers will "be afflicted and killed."

Being kept safe in this context means being kept from apostacy—denying the faith. Such apostacy is exactly what comes upon the many believers who betray their fellow believers, turn lawless and grow cold hearts. In this promise is the waring that if we don't doggedly purpose to go through everything faithfully, we too may become "offended" by what God allows the devil to do.

Meanwhile, one sign of enduring faith is that "the gospel of the kingdom" will at last go out to all the world, reaching every nation. This is not necessarily the "gospel of salvation" as great as that is but the message that this world has a kingdom that is coming in fullness and a King who is already ruling the universe. This focus of the gospel message is not about getting to heaven but bringing heaven down to earth through faith and obedience to earth's rightful King. It is the good news (gospel) of the coming kingdom.

As the Church aligns with its message and as that message is given a living witness, "the end will come." Which end does

---

4 Psalm 84:5-7 WEB

Jesus mean? Is this the end of the birth pains or the end of the Great Tribulation which only comes when He Returns—after its seven-year timespan? The prophetic picture is clearly that the harvest will continue throughout the Tribulation period with many unbelievers and Jewish believers coming to faith under the pressure of those events. Why would the Lord not want His best-trained disciples and most devoted followers "up in the air" when He needs them on the ground to help with the harvest?

7. The Abomination of Desolation

Therefore when you see the abomination of desolation, spoken of by Daniel the prophet, stand in the holy place (whoever reads, let him understand). Then let those in Judea flee into the mountains. Let him on the housetop not come down to take anything out of his house; nor let him in the field turn back to take his clothes. And woe to those who are with child, and to those who give suck in those days! But pray that your flight is not in the winter, nor on the sabbath day; Matthew 24:15-19 MKJV

This point on the timeline directly connects with Daniel's prophecy which describes the rule of the antichrist. This evil world ruler will be enthroned and worshiped in a rebuilt temple in Jerusalem. According to Daniel 12:11, when this event happens there will be 3 ½ years left before "the end of days."[5] Notice that Jesus, speaking to His disciples (and through them to us) says "when you see" this abomination taking place, then run for cover. How He describes that flight to safely is couched in the images of His day, but the key thing to note is that Jesus fully expects believers to see these things and take evasive action. There is nothing here to suggest that believers will already have been taken to safety (a Pre-Trib Rapture) or that Jesus will suddenly take them away now that this sign is revealed (a Mid-Trib Rapture). No. We will be here, and He will

---

[5] Daniel 12:11-13

not be coming to rescue us yet. We will, therefore, need to seek safety.

8. "Great" Tribulation Begins

For then shall be great tribulation, such as has not been since the beginning of the world to this time; no, nor ever shall be. And unless those days should be shortened, no flesh would be saved. But for the elect's sake, those days shall be shortened. Matthew 24:21-22 MKJV

It only gets worse. "Great tribulation" begins. It won't last forever—only for a while (those 3 ½ years mentioned above). While it lasts, however, Jesus says that it will be the worst the world has ever seen. Therefore, without a doubt this is the Great Tribulation which we all know is coming and which we all hope to escape or survive as the case may be. Our usual time for it is seven years, not three and a half.

Without opening up that debate, much less trying to resolve it, let's just take notice that Jesus doesn't say, "The great tribulation begins now" at this juncture where the abomination of desolation is revealed. He is simply saying that once this abomination stands in the temple, there will be "great tribulation." That is something everyone can agree on! Perhaps, this marks the mid-point of a tribulation that grew up as the birth pangs gained intensity. Perhaps, the seven-year persecution began at the point in the "sorrows" when persecution (tribulation) spread worldwide. In that case, we don't have a marker for the exact moment the seven-year Great Tribulation begins. At least not with this timeline. But we do have its mid-point. There will be no question about that exact moment: when the antichrist enthrones himself in a rebuilt temple in Jerusalem.

9. Deceived People and Deceptive Signs

Then if any man shall say to you, Lo, here is Christ! Or, There! Do not believe it. For false Christs and false prophets will arise and

show great signs and wonders; so much so that, if it were possible, they would deceive even the elect. Behold, I have told you beforehand. Therefore if they shall say to you, Behold, He is in the desert! Do not go out. Behold, He is in the secret rooms! Do not believe it. For as the lightning comes out of the east and shines even to the west, so also will be the coming of the Son of Man. For wherever the carcass is, there the eagles will be gathered. Matthew 24:23-27 MKJV

For the third time, Jesus warns against deception. Once more, false messages of hope will abound, spread by none other than the false prophet himself, along with false claims to be the savior everyone needs. Don't fall for it. No matter how badly believers will want Jesus to come, He's not coming early! So, He says, "Do not go out… Do not believe it." Nevertheless, even now—without any of these signs in place—without a temple and the antichrist in the temple, many believers are already running around expecting Jesus to come for His Bride *at any minute*. Are people not listening to what Jesus is so plainly saying?

Once again, through the disciples, Jesus is telling us that we will be on the ground during this time of persecution and tribulation. But we are to hold out in faith. He will not be coming secretly. When He comes everyone on earth will see Him just as we see lightning when it flashes "out of the east and shines even to the west." That moment hasn't yet arrived in this timeline, though it is just around the corner.

10. The Tribulation Ends with Darkness

And immediately after the tribulation of those days, the sun shall be darkened and the moon shall not give her light, and the stars shall fall from the heaven, and the powers of the heavens shall be shaken. Matthew 24:29 MKJV

This foreboding sign of darkness will also bring relief. It will certainly be a terrifying sign to unbelievers telling of their imminent doom. However, for those believers who have survived everything the antichrist and the devil threw at them, this darkening of the world will shout out that the Light of the World is about to appear. This will be like the drum roll which announces something big is about to happen.

Just as the beginning of a play is announced by bringing the house lights down, this darkening will claim everyone's attention and bring the whole chaotic world to silence. For those who have remained faithful, it will be a breathless silence filled with a heavenly anticipation. We will know that our "rapture" is about to occur. The Pre-Trib and Mid-Trib theories have that backwards, too. We won't be "taken" by surprise. Every one of us will feel the thrill in our hearts as the lights dim. We'll look up knowing that He is coming for us. And then…

11. Jesus Returns for All to See

And then the sign of the Son of Man shall appear in the heavens. And then all the tribes of the earth shall mourn, and they shall see the Son of Man coming in the clouds of the heaven with power and great glory. And He shall send His angels with a great sound of a trumpet, and they shall gather His elect from the four winds, from one end of the heavens to the other. Matthew 24:30-31 MKJV

The "sign" of the Son of Man appears! This word *sign* could easily be translated "supernaturally wondrous or miraculous." Don't think that it means our English word for something written in a secret code that requires interpretation. Not in this moment! All eyes will see Him. Jesus will be "coming in the clouds of the heaven with power and great glory."

That sight will be so stupendous a sign that no one could possibly miss it, even those who might wish they could, for "all the tribes of the earth"—the unbelievers who refused to acknowledge Him—will mourn. Their dismay will be great for it will be too late to receive Him now. On the other hand, those who have received Him and have been proven faithful, will hear that "the sound of a trumpet" and we will rise. Whether we are in "the heavens" (having died) or are still living under earth's "four winds," the angels will "gather His elect" to be with Him forever.

When does all this happen? After we go through the birth pains, after we go through the persecution and the perils, after the antichrist has his dark day, after the tribulation of those days, then "we will see" the Son of Man—Jesus—coming for His faithful Bride at last!

The Revelation Timeline

For the vision is yet for the appointed time,
and it hurries toward the end, and won't prove false.
Though it takes time, wait for it;
because it will surely come. It won't delay.

Habakkuk 2:3 WEB

THE REVELATION TIMELINE

Is there a coherent timeline of the Book of Revelation? Jesus gave us one in the gospels. It's recorded for us in Matthew Chapter 24. Wouldn't it be lovely if we could add another one to it, find where they match up and overlay them? That is exactly what John has given us! It's one more great reason to call him the "beloved" disciple—his "Revelation Timeline" will help us make sense of the maze of amazing events which he records for us in his vision. Evidently, the Lord had so much to show John (and tell us) that He couldn't fit it all into one single progression of events. Besides, we know from our own storytellers that it makes for a better movie if you throw in flashbacks, secondary narratives, and character development into the main plotline. John ingeniously did all this two millennia before Hollywood perfected it.

The revelation of Jesus Christ, which God gave him to show to his servants the things that must soon take place. Revelation 1:1

The Steady Succession of Judgments

If we limit the episodes in the Book of Revelation to the judgment sequences, the timeline swims into plain view. John stands in heaven's throne room for the entire succession of judgments and watches them from there. He is before God in company with the twenty-four elders and a host of angels the whole time. He does not have to move from this position for any of these events: the seals, the trumpets, and the bowls.

These events follow one another in a steady, unbroken succession from beginning to end. They proceed in an orderly sequence one right after the other. On heaven's side of things, we are not given any indication of the time passing. It is as if the seals are opened, the trumpet blasts get sounded, and the bowls are emptied all in a day. Yet, this is heaven's eternal day.

Many years pass in the course of these judgments—at least the seven years of the Tribulation and several years of the Birth Pains. Additionally, there is no stated indication that each judgment waits to follow only after the preceding one is completed. More likely, many, if not all, run on top of the time frame of the one that preceded it. In other words, although they occur in an orderly sequence, it is only the sequence of the beginnings we are shown, not the endings.

Despite these limitations, we have before us a timeline of tremendous importance. It runs from the beginning to the Birth Pains straight through to the very end of the judgments. Once the final bowl is poured there is nothing left, but to send in the invading army and claim the land. If we could pin it to a calendar at those two strategic points, then everything in between could be pulled and pushed back and forth like a slinky until each part lined up with an exact moment in time. We can trust the order for the beginning of each of these events that perfectly.

Additions to this Timeline

This timeline also perfectly matches the one set forth by Jesus on the Mount of Olives in Matthew 24. Jesus' timeline functions like a skeleton that gives us a framework—a broad outline. Its structure moves from Birth Pains, to the beginning of the worldwide Tribulation, to the mid-point of the antichrist's rise, through to the day of Return. The Revelation timeline fleshes out many of the prophesied judgments with graphic detail and shows us where they may be placed upon the bare bones Jesus supplied.

Curiously, the Seven Churches may have a place on this timeline, as well. As we've seen, their order exactly corresponded to the mail route which John's letter would have followed once it first arrived at Ephesus. Were they also listed by John (and Jesus) in the order that they would unfold in church history? It's just like the Lord to have planned things out that well. Although this is too complicated a study to go into here, if it's true, then it would set the beginning of this timeline in 90 AD.

The Revelation Timeline, therefore, could cover the entire future history of the church from the moment of its delivery to John into that far distant future which lies beyond the Millennium. In that case, the Laodicean Church would represent the seventh church age—the one that directly precedes the Birth Pains and Throne Room judgments.

Many believe that Laodicea exactly describes the lamentable condition of the church in our day. That brings us then, with this introduction and by our own current events, to the Successive Judgments. We will carry that timeline all the way through to the unveiling of the New Jerusalem with its River and Tree of Life. Chapter titles will be set in bold in the order that they appear on the timeline.

A Series of Judgments

The Throne Room

The vision literally takes off as John is transported to heaven. Emperor Domitian's reign (81-96 AD) is the likely period for John's exile to Patmos, especially towards the later years when persecutions launched by him grew in frequency and severity. Many commentators, therefore, would start the clock at about 95 AD in John's time.

The Sealed Scroll

The praise of heaven turns quickly to the serious business at hand—opening the scroll which contains the Last Days judgments. Only the Lamb Who Was Slain is worthy to open this scroll. We are entering into our own time with this transition from John's day.

The Four Horsemen

Seal 1: The rider on the white horse carries a bow, wears a crown, and goes forth "conquering and to conquer." In earth time, this would come near the beginning of the Birth Pains with an increase of conflicts between nations and ethnic groups.

> **The Matthew 24 Timeline:** Jesus said that "wars and rumors of wars… famines and earthquakes in various places… are but the beginning of the birth pains." Undoubtedly, that time begins with this rider, yet we have no indication of a calendar date. Note that He said the earthquakes would be in "various places." These are not the worldwide earthquakes of judgments still to come of which there will be four.

Seal 2: This one rides a red horse, carries a sword and "takes peace from the earth, so that people should slay one another." This indicates both civil disorder (in the wake of wars and other disasters) and an increase of violence of all kinds (no peace even within individuals).

Seal 3: The rider of the black horse carries scales which represents economic collapse leading to famine as the price of basic foods skyrocket. Since luxuries are not to be "harmed" it probably means that the wealthy elite will be untouched by these events.

Seal 4: Death and Hades ride forth (presumably) on separate pale horses to kill with sword and with famine and with pestilence and by wild beasts of the earth. They are working in tandem with the previous three horsemen, reaping their grim harvest. They have been given authority to bring death to "over a fourth of the earth." None of these riders have Christians or Jews specifically in their sights but persecutions will increase during this same period, building up to what we're shown next.

Seal 5: With this seal's opening we are clearly out of the Birth Pains. John sees under the altar "the souls of those who have been slain for the word of God and the witness they had borne." These are the martyrs of the Great Tribulation. The seven years have begun! The only question is how much time they had overlapped (if any) with the Birth Pains. Those pains would have included increasing waves of persecution against Christians and Jews, culminating in this worldwide pandemic of killing.

The Matthew 24 Timeline: These martyrs connect us directly to Jesus' timeline, though their appearance here doesn't give us an exact timestamp for its beginning. Even so, this greatest of all persecutions begins the seven-year period we commonly call the Great Tribulation. That so many martyred souls were under the altar shows us that the persecutions of the Tribulation were already well underway when John was shown this part of the vision. It is likely that the work of the riders in some way foments these persecutions, shifting the Birth Pains into becoming the Great Tribulation.

Concurrent Events: At the mid-point of the Tribulation, The First and Second Beasts will be fully, obviously in charge of world events (at least to our eyes). It is the antichrist's enthronement "in the holy place" –Jerusalem—that triggers the final half of the Tribulation which Jesus calls "great." At this mid-point, outbreaks of persecution which would have been taking place sporadically around the world, become an officially sanctioned policy of the one-world government.

This would also mark the emergence of The Mark of the Beast with its ruthless enforcement by the beast's image. During these final three and a half years, The Two Witnesses will be working out of Jerusalem and the offspring of The Woman will be seeking refuge from The Dragon. Additionally, only after the mid-point has passed will the

Beast have united his empire sufficiently to destroy The Harlot Babylon:

"And the ten horns that you saw, they and the beast will hate the prostitute. They will make her desolate and naked, and devour her flesh and burn her up with fire." Revelation 16:16

Seal 6: This opened seal triggers a "great earthquake" (the first of four) that darkens sun, moon, and stars and "removed from its place" every mountain and island. This judgment finally shakes the powerful and wealthy elites who seek to hide in fear from "the wrath of the Lamb."

Concurrent Events: Immediately following the opening of the Sixth Seal, we are shown The First 144,000 (along with others) who must be sealed on their foreheads before any further judgments may come. The Seventh Seal then leads into the Seven Trumpets

Seal 7: When the Lamb opens this seal there is silence in heaven for a half-hour, followed by prayers and incense at the altar. The prayers of the martyrs shown earlier are about to be answered. As an angel throws fire from the altar to the earth there are peals of thunder, rumblings, flashes of lightning, and yet another earthquake (the second). Seven angels now stand at the ready to blow their trumpets. Each trumpet will release yet more judgments.

The Revelation Timeline: Since the seals begin during the Birth Pains and stretch into the seven-year Tribulation, they take considerable time to unfold. One interpretation proposes seven years for the seals, seven months for the trumpets and seven days for the bowls. This seems reasonable, but what about this book has been reasonable so far? Still, the work of The Four Horsemen could easily cover the span of many years—from some point in the Birth Pains to deep inside the Great Tribulation.

Almost all the judgments which follow the first four seals could each happen in a single day, though those days don't have to occur back to back. We are told that the fifth trumpet judgment takes five months. The sixth trumpet, however, requires an unspecified amount of time. Nevertheless, with the immense number of demons involved (two billion), their killing spree could be over in a matter of days or weeks. That could leave only a week of judgments remaining as The Bowls of Wrath seem to be poured out in rapid-fire succession. Once, the series is complete, the King returns for the final battle, Armageddon.

The First Four Trumpets

Trumpet 1: When this trumpet sounds, "hail and fire, mixed with blood… were thrown upon the earth." This cataclysm burns a third of the earth.

Trumpet 2: As this note is struck, "something like a great mountain, burning with fire, was thrown into the sea and a third of the sea became blood." As a result, one-third of all sea creatures die, and one-third of all ships are destroyed.

Trumpet 3: When this angel blows his trumpet, "a great star fell from heaven, blazing like a torch." This lands on the earth and poisons a third of all freshwater, causing many to die. Its name is Wormwood.

Trumpet 4: With the fourth trumpet's sounding the sun, moon and stars are impacted "so that a third of their light might be darkened" during both day and night. This would likely be the partial obscuring of all celestial bodies due to an extensive debris cloud from the first three disasters.

It is entirely possible that these four events describe the double asteroid Apophis. If it indeed is on a collision course with the earth, the time of its arrival would be April 13, 2029. In that case, the breakup of smaller portions of a giant asteroid would account for the first trumpet's rain of fire from heaven. A double asteroid (such as Apophis) would account for the one-two punches shown by trumpets two and three and the debris cloud of the fourth trumpet.

> **Concurrent Events:** The Harlot's overthrow connects directly with the second of the Three Angel Messages in Revelation Chapter 14. These three woes are identical to the final three trumpets. John heard the angelic announcement right after seeing The Second 144,000 and just prior to witnessing The Harvest of the Earth. Keep in mind that the Harlot is not to be equated with Babylon. Babylon is the beast's system that covers the earth. The Harlot "is the great city that has dominion over the kings of the earth." That city (possibly New York) will be destroyed well in advance of Babylon's ultimate downfall.

Trumpets Five and Six

Trumpet 5: At this blast the first of three "woes" begin. A fallen angel descends to earth and "was given the key to the shaft of the bottomless pit" which, when opened, spews forth so much smoke that the skies are once again partially darkened. An enormous plague of locusts streams out with power to torment for five months "but not to kill" those who are not sealed with God's seal. Their king over them is named in Hebrew as Abaddon, or in Greek as Apollyon.

Trumpet 6: This trumpet launches the second woe: "four angels, who had been prepared for the hour, the day, the month, and the year, were released to kill a third of mankind." Two billion "mounted troops" (twice ten thousand times ten thousand) ride forth under their leadership. These demonic hordes are not to be confused with soldiers of any earth battle we could see, such as

Armageddon which only comes after the final judgment—the seventh bowl of wrath.

Concurrent Events: The final Harvest of the Earth certainly takes place here, though it may not be limited to this relatively brief time. All the Last Days events have been harvesting the earth ever since the Four Horsemen tore out of heaven when the seals were opened. Those grim reapers reduced the earth's population by one fourth.

This moment, however, accounts for a full third of the earth's remaining population being slain. In the Harvest chapter we are shown angels with sharp sickles; here we see hordes of demons doing the "dirty work." These two seemingly opposed views are easily reconciled if we take heaven's perspective as showing us who's really in charge of the Harvest.

The Seventh Trumpet

Trumpet 7: This one comes with an angelic proclamation: "In the days of the trumpet call to be sounded by the seventh angel, the mystery of God would be fulfilled." Both earth and heaven are impacted by it. In heaven the temple is thrown open; on earth "there were flashes of lightning, rumblings, peals of thunder, an earthquake [the third], and heavy hail." The main portent, however, is that it heralds the Seven Plagues and Bowls of Wrath are about to be poured out.

The Matthew 24 Timeline: This seventh trumpet should not be equated with the famous "Last Trumpet" Jesus spoke about as heralding His Return because that one sounds in the earth for all of us to hear. All seven of the trumpet judgments will only be heard in heaven. Even more telling, this last of the seven trumpets is sounded before the final Bowls of Wrath are poured. Jesus will not return until they are finished. It may only take seven days for those bowls to be emptied, but that will seem like a lifetime for people still on the earth.

The Seven Plagues

The seven plagues are added to the wrath of God which is already filling the bowls. That wrath upon sin and those who refuse to turn from it has been in "storage" since the beginning of the Rebellion. Hence, the plagues are the specific form that God's wrath will now take in real time. No one who is sealed by the Lord will be afflicted by these plagues. They are all specifically targeted at the unrepentant who have worshipped and served the beast.

The Seven Bowls

Bowl 1: This plague afflicts "the people who bore the mark of the beast and worshiped its image" with "harmful and painful sores."

Bowl 2: Poured into the sea, this plague makes the saltwater "like the blood of a corpse," killing every living thing in the sea.

Bowl 3: This one is poured over rivers and springs of water. They, too, become blood, rendering all freshwater toxic.

Bowl 4: As this is poured on the sun, fierce heat (waves of radiation and solar flares?) scorches people all over the earth.

Bowl 5: This is a plague of intense, absolute darkness, both physical and spiritual, yet "People gnawed their tongues in anguish and cursed the God of heaven."

The Matthew 24 Timeline: The Bowls of Wrath will have such a punishing effect that the persecution of Christians and Jews will cease. The unrepentant servants of the beast and his system will be scurrying for cover in desperate attempts to save their own lives. Accordingly, this plague of darkness is the most likely connection to the one Jesus described.

> **"Immediately after the tribulation [persecution] of those days the sun will be darkened, and the moon will not give its light, and the stars will fall from heaven, and the powers of the heavens will be shaken."** Matthew 24:29

Bowl 6: The emptying of this bowl dries up the river Euphrates preparing the way for armies to march upon Jerusalem and the last battle. Along with this, unclean spirits looking like frogs go forth from the mouth of the dragon and the two beasts (the false prophet and the antichrist) to bring powerful deception upon those who are summoned by them to Armageddon.

Bowl 7: When the seventh angel pours out this bowl into the air a loud voice announces that the judgments end with this one. There then followed "flashes of lightning, rumblings, peals of thunder, and a great earthquake such as there had never been since man was on the earth, so great was that [fourth] earthquake."

Jerusalem and other cities split or fall into ruin, including Babylon the Great (the beast's system of political, economic and religious power) which receives full and final wrath. Islands disappear below the waves and mountains also are brought low. Gigantic hailstones rain down upon the unrepentant who remain.

Concurrent Events: With the seventh bowl we are told that "God remembered Babylon the great, to make her drain the cup of the wine of the fury of his wrath." Draining a cup to the dregs implies that one has been drinking it all along. Indeed, the whole judgment series has been striking those who partied with Babylon's Harlot and served Babylon's beast. This climax is the moment when the beast's empire is utterly brought to ruin—all that's left is an army mustering in the field. The Harlot had been thrown down and trampled by the beast long before The Fall of Babylon arrived.

Closing Sequence

The Marriage Supper

When the last judgments have finally ended, we are shown a Bride that has "made herself ready" for the time of her Marriage Supper "has come." This is the one event on the sequence that is in the "wrong place." Wouldn't you know it? There are exceptions to every rule, especially with this book. To understand how her time is "almost but not yet" read the chapter. The meal and marriage will likely take place after Armageddon, not before.

The Returning King

Immediately after the aerial bombardment of the Seven Bowls of Wrath, Jesus mounts up with His army of angels. All that is needed is time for the rebel forces to emerge from their shelters and lay siege to Jerusalem. Their journey to Jerusalem began with the sixth bowl, so they may already be dug in around the holy city.

The Matthew 24 Timeline: Jesus told us that He would not be coming back until after the Tribulation ends and the last trumpet sounds. With that impossible-to-ignore "loud trumpet call," the elect will be gathered "from the four winds" (earth's "four corners") and from heaven. Paul filled in the detail that the dead will be raised first and those of us still living on the earth would rise with them to meet Jesus in the air (1 Thessalonians 4). From that point on, we will be with Him forever. This is the supreme moment when all the prophetic scriptures converge.

Armageddon

Jesus isn't coming back to take us up. He's coming down to take down the antichrist's assembled armies at Armageddon. That's Hebrew for the "mount of assembly" which points us to Jerusalem as the location for earth's final conflict before the Millennium of peace begins. Once that battle is over, Jesus will separate the sheep from the goats. Look for the Lamb to marry the sheep (us) once that judgment—the Judgment Seat of Christ—fully reveals who all of us are.

The Millennium Reign

The first act of Jesus' reign is to judge the nations, then be given in marriage by the Father to the Bride (though this is not spelled out in the text). These twin events must be settled first: that of casting the wicked to their reward and uniting His faithful Bride to Himself (as her reward). Then, the thousand years of peace unfold with earth's rightful King ruling in Jerusalem with His Wife at His side, reigning with Him.

The Very Last Battle

At the end of the thousand years, the Tempter is released from being bound in the bottomless pit to test those who have been born under the ideal conditions of the Millennium. Astonishingly, he manages to raise an immense army of people who should have known better. This leads to yet one more "last battle" which also takes place in the environs of Jerusalem. Don't be confused: One final conflict ends the church age, the other ends the Millennium.

The Last Judgment

This also is one of two. It's the second final judgment. The first launched the Millennium by bringing judgment to all who were still living on the earth when Jesus returned. That's generally called the Judgment Seat of Christ. This one, the Great White Throne judgment, comes after the Millennium. It will bring judgment to all those who lived and died before the Millennium began. That will be an incalculable number of people—far, far beyond the number of those who stood before Jesus.

New Heaven and Earth

By means of The Very Last Battle and The Great White Throne judgment, Satan, the rebel army of nations, and even Death and Hades are thrown into the lake of fire. This freeing of the earth from those who chose to reject God clears the way for the New Heavens, the New Earth, and the New Jerusalem to arrive. John does his best, but it's hard to describe things that have never been seen before—by anyone.

The New Jerusalem

With the New Jerusalem we are shown many marvels. The chief ones are the presence of both the Father and Jesus in our midst. Because of Their presence we will live inside the glory that radiates throughout the holy city. There will be no further need of sun or moon for our God(s) will supply all the light the Bride will ever need. The other marvel is the identity of the immense multitude of pilgrims streaming in from the provinces. Hint: They are not the Bride.

The River and the Tree

Right in the center of the New Jerusalem are two extraordinary features that carry us full circle to the Garden of Eden which had a life-giving river flowing through it and a tree of life within it. As we will see one Day in that great by and by, the River of Life is the life-sustaining presence of the Holy Spirit and the Tree of Life is the life-giving presence of our Lord Jesus.

Forerunner Ministries

*Which hope we have
as an anchor of the soul,
both sure and steadfast,
and which enters into that within the veil,
where the Forerunner has entered for us, even Jesus.*

Hebrews 6: 19-20a MKJV

APPENDIX D

FORERUNNER MINISTRIES

Seeking to serve the Lord Jesus as He works to:

1. Reach the lost.
2. Cleanse and heal His Bride.
3. Reveal the Father's glorious love.
4. Prepare the Church for what is coming.
5. Release the glorious liberty of His children.

THE eCOURSE FOR HEALING
www.HealingStreamsusa.org

Practically everyone needs recovery of their heart from some painful issues of the past or could readily benefit from gaining mastery over their emotional turbulence in the present. The peace of Christ is meant to be a river of life that we experience all day long—no matter what our circumstances may be. Let the 24 main healing lessons and workout sessions of our free eCourse for Healing take your heart on pilgrimage to a place called the Kingdom of God that is already right inside you.

SPIRIT FILLED LIVING IN CHRIST
www.Forerunners4Him.org

Whether you are a brand new recruit or a "seasoned veteran," if you find that your peace levels are slipping and your joy is not full, then everything on this site is designed to help you come into the fullness of what it truly means to be saved by grace through faith— in all of your days and all of your situations. For us a forerunner is anyone who receives salvation and begins a lifetime quest of "running" into the Heart of God for intimacy and "going before the Lord" to prepare His way into other lives. That's your heart too, isn't it? Come get the equipping you need to be a liberated lover of Jesus and a loving liberator of others.

SANE AND SENSIBLE PERSPECTIVES
www.TheLastDays.info

Many people these days have a God-given hunger to know more about the Last Days. You'll find a feast at this website! Savor the taste of these "sane and sensible perspectives" which are salted with humor and spiced with fresh insights. We have extensive sections devoted to Signs of His Coming, When Is the Rapture, Crucial Components, and Ways to Prepare along with free downloads, an Updates section and blog. Best of all, an entire six-hundred-page commentary on The Book of Revelation is available for free reading and chapter by chapter download.

BOOKS FROM FORERUNNER

If you enjoyed this book, you can purchase copies for friends and keep exploring the spiritual life through these other insightful books by Steve Evans, available in paperback and eBook at Amazon.com.

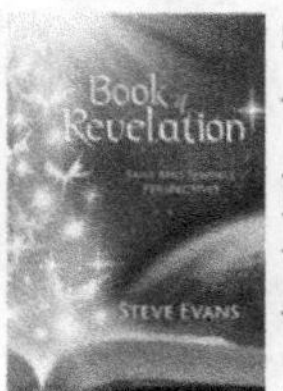

The Book of Revelation takes you on a verse-by-verse stroll through the most complex prophetic vision ever given. These "sane and sensible perspectives" are guaranteed to help you see what this amazing book is trying to show us. With this detailed overview, you'll have the insights you'll need for the days to come.
624 pages. Paperback: $22.00. Kindle: $3.99.

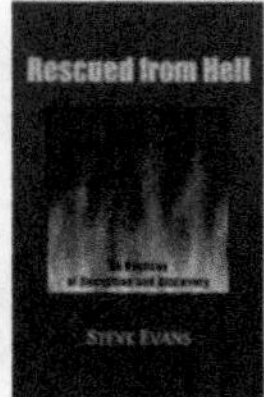

Rescued from Hell chronicles one man's journey into a ten-year living nightmare and his astonishing true story of return. Was it an insane delusion or a satanic deception? This is a tale both incredible and terrible, yet studded with life affirming humor and hope-filled insights into the spiritual realities that surround us.
190 pages. Paperback: $12.50; Kindle: $2.99.

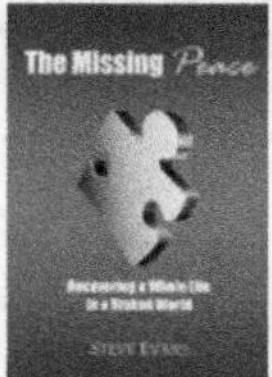

The Missing Peace includes all 24 lessons of the ***Matters of the Heart*** teaching series, but without the workbook's other material, focusing instead on a stream of scriptural revelation that will show you how to bring your heart to God and receive His Heart for you in return. You can recover from past emotional damage!
194 pages. Paperback: $15.00; Kindle: $2.99.

Jesus: An Intimate Portrait will give you fresh perspectives on His Story—the heroic story of the One who shapes all human history by His life and Word. Let these intimate insights reveal the living, breathing God-Man in ways you never encountered Him before. Seeing Him changes everything!
212 pages. Paperback: $15.00; Kindle: $2.99.

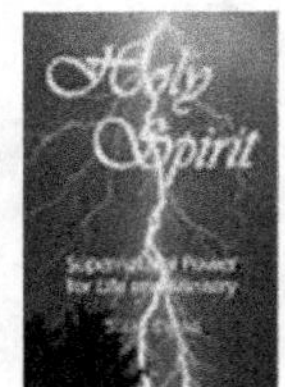

Holy Spirit explores practical ways of getting to know the One who supplies us with supernatural power for life and ministry. Why should the Person of the Trinity who lives within us be so mysterious to us? This book combines ***Knowing the Spirit*** with ***Ministry Basics*** in a single, sensational volume.
171 pages. Paperback: $15.00; Kindle: $2.99.

Matters of the Heart is a 24 lesson workbook designed to guide Christian believers through the basic understandings necessary for releasing emotional damage from the past and gaining a grace-based restoration to wholeness. Each chapter is filled with "tools" for practical application.
278 pages. Paperback: $20.00; Kindle: $2.99.

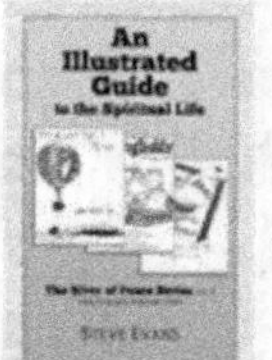

An Illustrated Guide to the Spiritual Life captures in living color with playful insights the otherwise elusive, invisible realities of our life in God. This "illustrated devotional" includes explanations, scriptures and prayers. It is written for the general reader, but is also a pictorial companion to ***The Missing Peace***.
126 pages. Paperback: $17.50; Kindle: $2.99.
The River of Peace Series, Vol. 1.

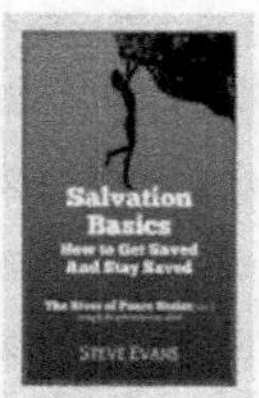

Good Grief is not for everyone, but for those who despite their pain have "set their hearts on pilgrimage," determined to make it faithfully to the other side of the Valley of Tears, by allowing sorrow that is *rightly* carried to mend their hearts and guide them toward God's new beginning.
176 pages. Paperback: $10.00; Kindle: $2.99.
The River of Peace Series, Vol. 2.

Salvation Basics provides easy to understand answers to life's most important questions: "What will happen to me when I die?" and "What can I do about it?" You will not only discover God's grace-filled way for getting you to heaven, but also His "secret" for living the heavenly life down here.
118 pages. Paperback: $10.00; Kindle: $2.99.
The River of Peace Series, Vol. 3.

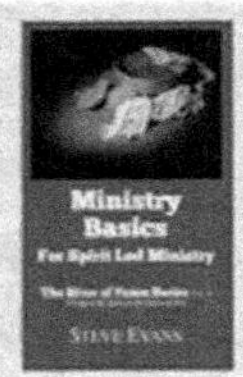

Ministry Basics will prepare you to launch into the sea of human need, lostness and misery which surrounds you, finding your place in the Rescue and your highest path of purpose at the Lord's side. Let these field-tested truths equip you for a joy-filled lifetime of Holy Spirit empowered ministry.

163 pages. Paperback: $10.00; Kindle: $2.99.

The River of Peace Series, Vol. 4.

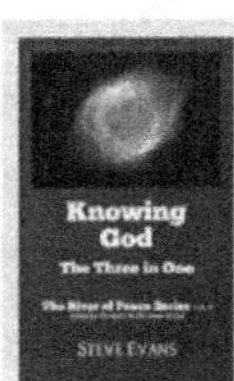

Knowing God may surprise you. The invisible God can be truly, intimately and delightfully known. But it gets even better because there are not just One of Him to get to know, but Three. Think of this as a guide book, not an encyclopedia. Three amazing Persons already know you and love you. What are you waiting for?

161 pages. Paperback: $10.00; Kindle: $2.99.

The River of Peace Series, Vol. 5.

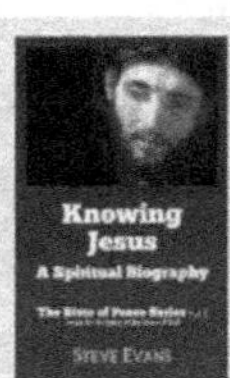

Knowing Jesus will introduce you to the God-Man. He is far and away the most wonderful Person in the universe to know. And He can be known! Simply opening one's heart to Him is all He needs for that life-long adventure to begin. Let this "Spiritual Biography" lead you into fresh revelations of key moments in His life.

159 pages. Paperback: $10.00; Kindle: $2.99.

The River of Peace Series, Vol. 6.

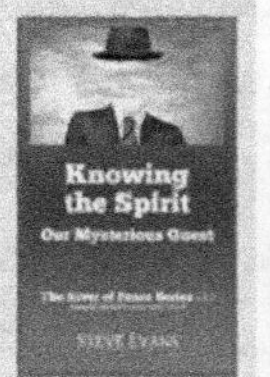 ***Knowing the Spirit*** will introduce you to the Mystery Person of the Trinity, help you recognize His ways and connect with His presence, so that you can live with greater delight in His guidance and power. Let this book give you eyes to see and ears to hear your inner Guest as He works with you each day.

149 pages. Paperback: $10.00; Kindle: $2.99.

The River of Peace Series, Vol. 7.

ABOUT THE AUTHOR

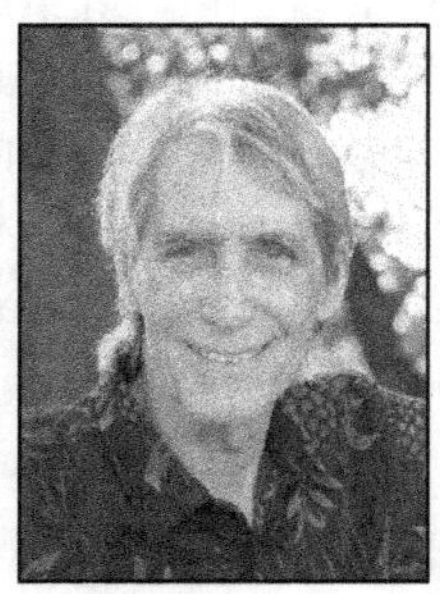

Steve Evans came to faith as one brought back from the dead after a decade of occult oppression and torment. His passion is to see people everywhere released from past brokenness and fully equipped for life and ministry. At HealingStreamsUSA.org he teaches believers how to recover their emotional freedom and master their inward state. At Forerunners4Him.org he shows how to live in the presence and power of the Spirit. His newest website, TheLastDays.info, gives "sane and sensible perspectives" on the events of the Last Days that are heading our way.

Steve has authored numerous books, including: *The Missing Peace, The Book of Revelation, Salvation Basics, Good Grief, Knowing Jesus* and *Rescued from Hell* which tells the story of his own harrowing descent into inner darkness and ultimate restoration. Steve is an ordained minister and a former carpenter, craftsman and missionary.

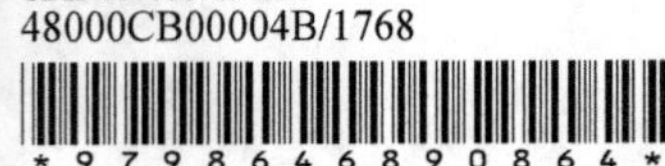